~ A PASSION FOR ~

FLOWERS

PENNY BLACK

~ A PASSION FOR ~

FLOWERS

PENNY BLACK

SIMON AND SCHUSTER

New York · London · Toronto · Sydney · Tokyo · Singapore

DEDICATION
Remembering my parents and a uniquely rich childhood.

SIMON AND SCHUSTER
Simon and Schuster Building
Rockefeller Center
1230 Avenue of the Americas
New York, New York 10020

Published simultaneously in Great Britain by Ebury Press, an imprint of the Random
Century Group

Edited by GILLIAN HASLAM AND EMMA CALLERY
Designed by PETER BRIDGEWATER
Photographs by JACQUI HURST
Illustrations by LORRAINE HARRISON

Typeset in Bembo by Textype Typesetters, Cambridge
Printed and bound in Italy by New Interlitho S.p.a., Milan

10 9 8 7 6 5 4 3 2 1

Library of Congress Cataloguing in Publication Data Available Upon Request

ISBN: 0–671–75106–9

ACKNOWLEDGMENTS

I would like to thank everyone who encouraged me to contemplate this book, and all those who gave me the freedom to do it in the manner that came most naturally to me. My agent, Shan Morley Jones is always a pillar of support and I thank her for her quiet wisdom. Everyone at Ebury Press has been a delight to work with; Amelia Thorpe and Gillian Haslam appreciated my persuasion from the outset and encouraged me to follow it; my editor, Emma Callery, has at all times shown sensitivity towards, and an understanding of, my text and it has been a privilege to work with her, and Jacqui Hurst, whose talent is reflected in the photographs in the book, introduced me to a perception of beauty and detail that is quite different to my own and it has been an inspiration to work with such a talented photographer. Of course, there are many others who I would like to thank and they include Tony and Eira Hibbert for the fronds of the New Zealand tree fern and hydrangea blossoms; Angela Sheldon-Fentem for the loan of antique textiles; Peter and Mollie Whitbread for allowing us to photograph their barn; Kathie Thomas for helping me bring the garden back under control and my dear family, who are always patient and supportive.

SUPPLIERS

Arts and Graphics, 4 West End, Redruth, Cornwall TR16 5ND (papers and art materials); Jill Cadnam, Handmade Papers, 6 The Old Boys School, Illogan, Churchtown, Redruth, Cornwall TR16 4SW (handmade Indian paper); Global Village (garden furniture); Victoria Hilliard, Bosavern Mill, Cot Valley, St Just, Cornwall TR19 7NT (painted relief butterfly picture); Jackie Phillips Flowers, 6 The Moor, Falmouth, Cornwall (flowers).

CONTENTS

❧ I N T R O D U C T I O N   6

❧ S P R I N G   14
Bluebells *18* • Decorated Screen *22* • Crystalized
Spring Flowers *24* • Cauldron of Spring
Potpourri *26* • Collage of a Vase of Flowers *30* •
Islamic-style Pressed Flower Pictures *34* •
Skeletonized Collage *37* • Arrangement of Spring
Grasses in a Tin Hat Box *39* • Botanical Herb
Picture *41* • Stripes *45*

❧ S U M M E R   46
Twiggy Cupboard *51* • A Wedding Garland *52* •
Herbs in the Kitchen *54* • Flowery Candles *57* •
Indian Patchwork Collage *59* • Summer Rose
Potpourri *60* • A Basket of Lavender *65* •
Oriental Poster *68* • Bottles on a Sleeper *71* •
Flowerpot Collage *73* • Three-dimensional
Picture *75*

❧ A U T U M N   76
Dried Hydrangeas *81* • Indian Collage Cards *83* •
Anemone Potpourri in a Decorated Tin Box *85* •
Basket of Autumn Botanicals *86* • An Ironstone
Pitcher of Flowers *89* • Red Paneled Picture *92* •
Large Posy of Flowers *95* • Vetiver Garlands and
Potpourri-filled Boxes *97* • Tumbling Bouquet
100 • Autumn Leaves *105*

❧ W I N T E R   106
Black and White Arrangement *110* • Snowdrop
Candelabra *112* • Sunflower Heads, Docks and
Patchwork *114* • Seaweed Picture *117* • Borders
121 • Basket of Silvered Fruit and Seedheads *124*
• Lichen-covered Branches *126* • Nest of
Flower-Decorated Brown Boxes *128* • Lichen
Garland *131* • Cornish Anemones on a Tartan
Rug *132* • Moss-covered Basket of Dried
Flowers *135*

Pressing and Drying Plants   *141*
A Seasonal Guide to Suitable Plants for Pressing and Drying   *142*
Common Plants and Their Scientific Names   *143*
Index   *144*

INTRODUCTION

*M*y earliest memories are strewn with posies of snow-drops, primroses, violets, wild daffodils and summer's bluebells, and their tender beauty always reminds me of the ecstasies of a country childhood. The small thatched cottage where I whiled away those early years lay deep within a lichen-covered orchard in a countryside of fields, thick hedgerows, watermeadows and woods. I was left free to wander at will through this abundant landscape and I slowly became intimate with an exquisite and exciting world. The spell that was cast over my perception so many years ago has never lost its potency and the solitude of a wood carpeted with pale anemones still enraptures me, as does the fragrance of a bedroom filled with the cool scent of a dew-laden night, or the arrival of the first swallow.

> *I made a posy, while the day ran by:*
> *Here will I smell my remnant out, and tie*
> *My life with this band.*
>
> GEORGE HERBERT

The countryside's rich tradition of plant and folklore has also been my inheritance. The indoctrination has been such that I still quake when the twisting stems of poison-berried bryony, yew berries, lethal hemlock or brown-flowered deadly nightshade cross my path, and the sickly scent of hawthorn fills me with unease. I like to plant myrtle by the side of the front door simply because I was told that it would ensure the happiness of the family within and I regret that rowan does not grow by the cottage gate, for I am still enchanted by the concept that it will keep away the evil spirits! Perhaps deep within my psyche there lurks a belief in natural magic for certainly as a child I lived within the rules that it imposed.

From a very early age I had a small patch of garden where I sowed poppy, night-scented stocks, pea and bean seeds. By the time I was nine years old, I had reclaimed part of the orchard as my own and grew any plant that caught my eye. I was not knowledge-able in the naming of any but the most common flowers, but was extremely intimate with the requirements, mode of growth, structure and perfume of many plants. Today it is still the character of a plant that will fascinate me more than its beauty within a border, which is perhaps why I garden in such an abandoned style.

PREVIOUS PAGE
This Victorian hand-
cart is filled to
overflowing with huge
bouquets of mixed
flowers gathered from
my summer garden.
Armfuls of mixed
blooms, from the
prettiest pink
meadowsweets, lime-
green lady's mantle,
spireas, mauve-
flowered woolly mints,
astilbes, trailing
wands of clematis and
lysimachias to
summer's earliest
hydrangeas are
crammed into buckets
of water. The effect is
very free and
outstandingly lovely.

Over the years I have forged ahead with a style of gardening that emanates from a love of flowers and follows no fashion. My husband well understands the imagery that fires my plantings and his artistic concept of an overall design has enabled me to create, together with my immense band of wild and cultivated plants, a visually exciting garden that follows no rules nor accepted style. I love the flowers for what they are and I mix them together quite indiscriminately, only hoping that they will thrive and be happy. I would add that I do take account of texture in the garden and will go to infinite trouble to obtain and place interesting and unusual foliage plants.

Other aspects of my childhood have also had a profound influence over my adult life and I am always aware of the rich contribution that was made by my parents. They filled our home with the decorative arts and collected with the ardor of magpies. The cottage glistened with treasures, and paintings, embroideries and antique textiles decorated the crumbling walls. Our everyday china was chipped and exquisitely decorated and unusual objets d'art were crammed on every surface. Of course I took it all for granted and did, in fact, yearn for a home that was more conventional! My mother was an outstanding needlewoman and together we explored the intricacies of fine sewing and embroidery. I cannot remember a day when I was not as fascinated by a Banksian stitched rose as I was by the real thing. In fact, so much has the world of flowers and gardening been integrated with that of embroidery, appliqué, silks and satins that I often think that my garden looks more like an embroidery and my embroidery and collages more like a garden.

The smells, both fragrant and otherwise, of childhood remain within me, too. They were a familiar but intangible ingredient of my earliest contemplation of life within the cottage and surrounding countryside. The fragrance of oil lamps and candles filled every nook and cranny of our home, just as the mysterious perfume of incense penetrated everything in the church where I worshiped. Iodine was dabbed on every childhood wound and I still find its antiseptic smell irresistible as I do the fragrance of coal-tar soap. Eucalyptus and lavender scented my handkerchiefs and newly ironed linen smelled of fresh air. Grandma sent wafts of eau-de-cologne and mothballs across the room and my mother's face was sweetly perfumed with the peachy powder that she applied to her nose. When I was close to my father I could smell tobacco and engine oil and an auntie was reassuringly redolent with the musky smell of the young animals that she so loved. In the garden and countryside there were rank smells which I hated, but also lots of lovely perfumes. I like the smell of trampled water mint and thyme as much as I ever did and the fragrance of primroses, bluebells, clove-scented roses and pink and white violets remain the sweetest perfumes of childhood. The recollection of a smell is very accurate and elder leaves and wood, crushed ivy and many of the poisonous plants smell as bitter and rank now as they did when I encountered them during my early years. Our lives are full of scents and those that recall the past reinforce the structure of one's life. Such is my fascination that I now like to delve more deeply into the world of scent and more particularly into the romantic history of perfume.

Behind the cottage is a steep wooded bank. Sheltered and damp, it is a natural haven for mosses in great variety, pennyworts and ferns. This thick carpet of Aulacomnium andrognum *runs down the bank and tumbles either side of an old sycamore tree, coating its gnarled roots with a spongy green blanket. The moss is fluorescent emerald green and studded with succulent, mildly glaucous, pennywort leaves.*

I moved to Cornwall with my family fifteen years ago and it had taken us a long time to find a cottage with land and enough potential to fulfil our dreams. The small river crossed by an old granite footbridge was an unexpected bonus, but little did we realize how the Trethellan Water was to influence and change our entire concept of gardening. There was no garden as such when we moved in, just a small overgrown terrace, and a field of docks, thistles and rushes. Other than two old Monterey pines there were no trees either, and during the winter of 1976/77 the winds from the Atlantic blew relentlessly across our land. The Cornish rain fell ceaselessly too, flooding the river and transforming the lower field into a bitter swampland.

I had brought to Cornwall some 400 plants and was eager to find temporary homes for them. I planted the old roses in what I believed to be a field, but they were washed away when the river

12

PREVIOUS PAGE
These are the flower
borders in the lower
garden, overflowing
with moisture-loving
Asiatic plants. The
sheer abundance of
growth in the rich
damp soil is
overwhelming, and
each year I forget just
how beautiful the vista
through the trees and
along the winding
grass paths is. In a
matter of two weeks,
the area is
transformed into the
most beautiful
paradise of primulas,
irises, rheums, ferns,
mints, ranunculas,
hostas, azaleas and
rhododendrons.

flooded and a new watercourse raged across the low-lying land. My collection of campanulas slowly declined in the mists, wind and rain, and the Mediterranean plants died as quickly as I planted them. Even my old primroses, which had actually indicated that they quite liked Cornwall, were one day ravaged by marauding bantams. I was sad and confused, for the dreams of a garden were collapsing before my eyes. But I was to learn much during the coming years and as the phoenix rose from the ashes, so our garden burgeoned and blossomed from an inhospitable and wet moorland becoming a verdant plantsmans' Utopia.

I discovered that we were blessed with a rich, moist, acid soil and that water draining from the fields above the cottage ran continually through our garden and into the river. The watertable is never, even in the driest summer, far beneath the surface of the soil. I knew nothing of the Cornish climate and was surprised to find that the air remains moist throughout the year, even more so in close proximity to a river, small though it may be. I also discovered that nothing over 6 inches high could survive unless given some shelter from the prevailing south-westerly winds. And so along our boundary we planted swamp cyprus, alders, willows in great variety, cornus, viburnum and oak. They grew like ferns in the rich, wet and often flooded soil and within three or four years our summer garden became more sheltered. I was not familiar with the perennials that like damp, acid conditions and so I started from the beginning and researched all that I could about them. I planted seeds by the thousand and bought as many plants as I could afford. I took cuttings of azaleas and layered friends' rhododendrons and camelias. To help finance the garden I potted up and sold all my surplus seedlings and rooted cuttings of the established shrubs. Gradually a beautiful Asiatic garden evolved and I would never now change our damp, and often mist-shrouded, slopes for the conditions of a more conventional garden. We have become quite used to the flooding of the river. In fact, the lower borders remain underwater for most of the winter, but now the plants in that area thrive, and during the summer their growth is rampant. Almost all the plants disappear underground during the winter and only emerge as the sun warms the earth and opens the leaves of the sheltering trees. It is at this time that the immense fertility of the garden manifests itself and delectable plants from China, Tibet, Nepal and Japan bloom in profusion. But, of course, it is the British wild and cottage-garden flowers that remain my first love, and I allow all those tolerant of the garden's conditions to hobnob with the aristocrats in wanton profusion.

I love the colour of the columbines that are not quite white. Some of the petals are edged with palest pink, some with milky blue and others with the softest green. As dusk falls, the drooping pale flowers remain suspended over the dark herbage of the borders.

I have been making potpourris, herb pillows and scented sachets for a long time, but it is only during the last six years that I have experimented with pressed flowers. After a great deal of experimentation I now find that I can create collages of flower-filled baskets, cottage posies, decorative botanical posters and totally freestyle pictures with relative ease. In this book I have explored lots of other styles and hope that I have demonstrated how ideas can be plucked from the most unlikely source of inspiration. Looking back I realize that I have served a lifetime's apprenticeship in 'all things botanical' and that my collages are the distillation of all the visual pleasures of my life.

During the course of this last year I have kept a diary of the garden and countryside. At the close of each season I have sat down with my notes and written of the flowers as I saw them, the changing nature of the garden and, of course, the vagaries of the Cornish weather. Even the animals, birds and insects have played their part and I have had immense pleasure in writing about it all. The collages, potpourris, and flower and botanical arrangements have also reflected the seasons and I have loved traveling along the unknown road of discovery as I searched for new and unusual ingredients and styles. I also realize how the dedication that I gave to this book has sharpened my awareness of the natural world. I look at my garden and the surrounding countryside more keenly now than ever before. Perhaps in knowing that I was to write about it, all the sensual delights of my life were released. I hope all who read this book will catch a glimpse of the garden and landscape that has been my inspiration.

PART ONE

SPRING

'*Sweet Spring came dancing o'er a*
daisied lawn,
At break of dawn,
Tossing her aery curls in disarray
From a wreath of May.'
ED STONE

16

Our Cornish garden lies in a small valley that runs along the lower edge of ancient moorland. Beneath the rich black soil, and forming the foundations of the cottage, rests a long, cold finger of granite. This crystalline rock keeps the winter soil temperature quite low and sunshine must warm the earth of our garden, and the valley too, before spring flowers appear in their immense profusion. Sheltering willows, alders, blackthorns, hawthorns and sycamores remain leafless long after trees at sea level are showing green, and this also ensures that our spring is late and slow. I love this tardy quickening of the season. Often, late winter flowers bloom with those of spring, and snowy rivers of lawn daisies can glisten with the last of the celandines. In a haze of silver-blue, speedwell can engulf late snowdrops, and in the pond, Caucasian kingcups can bloom alongside arum lilies. In the soggy, bare flower borders, the huge clumps of moisture-loving plants emerge with caution.

> *Oh year grow slowly, exquisite, holy,*
>   *The days go on*
> *With almonds showing the pink stars blowing,*
>   *And birds in the dawn.*
>
> *Grow slowly year, like a child that is dear,*
>   *Or a lamb that is mild,*
> *By little steps, and by little skips,*
>   *Like a lamb or a child.*

KATHERINE TYNAN

Gradually, the earth is spotted yellow-green and with the emergence of this new growth the air in the garden softens and smells faintly of a bouquet of fresh spring leaves. Imperceptibly the grass in the field which lies opposite the cottage lengthens, and I am suddenly aware that when ruffled by the wind it has become a shimmering meadow.

It is now that paling celandines lose the lacquer of their petals; flurries of stitchwort and mauve dog violets stain the hedgerows; campions and herb Robert are out in the wilder parts of the garden, and large, rusty-rumped bumblebees and demure honeybees plunder the first flowers. Fragile early spring has established herself in my garden; no longer need I dream of her countenance for my landscape is embroidered with her delicate beauty. Leaf by leaf, and blossom by blossom, my garden is slowly transformed into a green-washed paradise of flowers.

Early morning sunshine falls across the lower garden. Lusty candelabra primulas are in bloom and the Royal fern is uncurling its giant, smooth fronds. Day lilies and Sanguisorba canadensis *are already 2-ft (60-cm) mounds but* Polygonum campanulatum *is still creeping along the ground gathering strength for a magnificent late summer display of lacy white blossoms. Kingcups and skunk cabbage are out and soon the beautiful blossoms of the* Iris kaemperi *will be hovering above their broad and fragile strap-like leaves.*

When the sun is out it is deliciously warm on the face, but when dark clouds race in from the west, obscuring the early spring sun, there is an icy nip to the air. Swarms of winter gnats are still around and the gentle warbling and chattering of the birds is lazy and without motivation. The earliest self-sown seeds are germinating and I notice that the large cotyledon leaves of honesty are scattered ever further over the garden. I love honesty, mauve or white, and even more so do I like the variegated forms. In twilight, the spectral beauty of the white-flowered variety can be seen from afar. It should be planted in a night garden, for its fragrance is stronger at dusk and during the night.

The delicate lilac blossoms of *Primula vulgaris sibthorpii* are out. It is a tough little early-flowering primrose, almost indestructible, and should be grown in more gardens. On the terrace, the first speedwells are palely flowering. Their quick-dropping fragile blooms go straight to my heart for the lawns of my childhood were dusted with them. The succulent, knobbly cones of grape hyacinth blossoms are still deep within their rosettes of leaves, but they mature quickly, and if there is sunshine they will shoot up and turn blue in a matter of days. The streamers of the *Clematis armandii*, looping and twining around the roses, akebia, vines, and ivies of the barn, are carrying tight, translucent packages of blossoms that are just longing to emerge and fill the air with their sweet perfume. A few more days of sunshine and they will do just that.

For some unknown reason my cowslips, who hate the wet acid soil of the garden, always bloom incredibly early. The small clump is in bloom during the earliest weeks of spring and they stand, long-legged and shoulders back, bowing their demure freckled bells. I have to jump into the middle of the flower border to smell them, but smell them I must, for my early memories are embalmed in their sweet perfume. If I was able to grow more I would have cowslip pancakes for tea and make cowslip wine.

To understand the historical significance of plants, it is necessary to delve into their past. The earliest botanists were magicians and all plants were believed to possess magical qualities. Through them, good or evil could be evoked and all the sickness, fears, doubts, questions and desires of the frail human mind and body could be dealt with. They held the answer to life or death, happiness or despair, and their effects were manipulated through the mystical psychic powers of magicians, witches, priests, sorcerers, wizards and even necromancers.

These powerful, feared and often respected botanists believed that the purpose and properties of each herb were decreed by a sign within the plant itself. This was known as the Doctrine of Signatures, a knowledge of which leads to a greater understanding of the history of many of our old plants. Hence, because of the cowslips' freckles, an infusion of that same flower would cause freckles to vanish. Lungwort, whose spotted leaves resemble lungs, would cure all pulmonary ailments; barrenwort, bladderwort, birthwort, staunchwort, and many others, are all self-explanatory in their curative properties. As well as the healing "worts" there were destructive "banes". Wolfsbane, cowbane (water hemlock dropwort that grows so profusely in my garden), henbane and fleabane are but just a few of the plants believed to kill the creature to which they refer, which indeed they often did. Hound's tongue was used to silence dogs, and viper's bugloss, with seeds like a wriggling snake, to relieve snake bites. All nonpoisonous plants with a milky juice were believed to promote a copious supply of milk; and plants containing a red juice would purify the blood. There was no limit to the imaginative use and naming of plants. Some of the ancient beliefs have stood the test of time for many of the plant drugs of today are used for the same purpose as they were used, in their unrefined state, centuries ago.

I love to wander around my garden and sniff the sneeze-wort, tweek the old man, wince at the birthwort or perhaps wonder if I should pick a bunch of fleabane and hang it over the cat's basket. William Shakespeare was very intimate with the nature of plants and put total faith in their power, as he indicated when he wrote:

Within the infant rind of this weak flower
Poison hath residence, and medicine power.

As I walk down our lane, the night sky is pale and the stars just tiny pinpricks, but for Venus who shines large and golden. Streaks of a waxing moon can be seen through the leafless branches of a Cornish cut-leafed oak, fat with buds. The night air is redolent with the earthy fragrance of an early spring night. In the uppermost branches of two old Monterey pines standing alongside the bottom of our drive, large twiggy nests have already been refurbished in readiness for spring broods. Honking and irritable crows will be the first to rear their fledglings, waking me before first light. Pigeons are fickle in their choice of a nesting site and will make several false starts elsewhere, but will inevitably return to the storm-ravaged, uppermost branches of the pines. A goldcrest is building her pendulous, mossy nest among the wiry foliage. During early spring she gathers the cobwebs that hang around the cottage windows from where I can study her in detail. I always feel intensely curious and rather excited when I encounter her, for she is even smaller than the Jenny Wren and her little eyes are so penetrating. Sometimes a woodpecker will drum away at the rough wood and then fly off uttering his distinctive "kik kik kik".

I have tried many times to grow roses and ivies up the massive trunks of the pines, but nothing seems to survive the poor soil around their base. Interestingly, a wild ivy has crawled over a nearby bank and it has clambered at least 20 feet up into the largest of the two trees. I would never have thought of planting my roses and ornamental ivies quite so far away from their host trees.

Carpets of sweet woodruff grow profusely in the garden. When picked, the leaves slowly release the fragrance of coumarin, or new mown hay, as they dry.

CRYSTALIZED SPRING FLOWERS

FOR years I have decorated cakes for special occasions with posies of crystalized spring flowers and herbs. Butter icing can be flipped around in unsophisticated mounds and waves, colored in delicate hues and then decorated with pastel blue forget-me-nots, mauve violets, alabaster-white daisies and delicious tiny leaves of sweet Cicely, mints, rosemary and even small strawberry leaves.

Always use edible flowers (you will find that many herbals and cookery books list them) and herbs.

To crystalize them, lightly beat the white of an egg and then, using a fine artist's brush, coat the flowers and leaves with egg white. Sift caster sugar over them and dry in a very low oven, leaving the door ajar.

The small tea table is in front of the 'herb border', home to the herbs used to decorate the cake. The tiny cut-glass and silver vase contains coveted mauve-pink lily-of-the-valley, exactly the same shade as the butter icing and pretty old china.

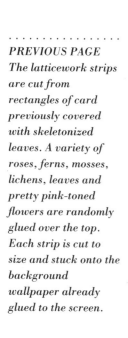

PREVIOUS PAGE The latticework strips are cut from rectangles of card previously covered with skeletonized leaves. A variety of roses, ferns, mosses, lichens, leaves and pretty pink-toned flowers are randomly glued over the top. Each strip is cut to size and stuck onto the background wallpaper already glued to the screen.

Ebony, our little black cat, has been in a state of dormouse hibernation most of the winter. Her shining coat is silky and thin and ruffles easily in the wind, exposing her delicate milk-white skin. Cats from the Orient cannot come to terms with wet, blustery, Cornish winters and so, even though there are a few birds, shrews and voles around, it is far better to sleep the inclement season through, emerging night and morning for sustenance. But now the quiet cold garden has started to change: the air is a little warmer, there is activity among the newly sprouting herbage, and sparrows chatter in the eaves. A micro-moth and lacewing fly have been caught in a web in the bathroom, a snail has appeared on the frame of a picture in our bedroom, and a few bees have buzzed into the cottage. And there are stirrings within our little cat too. Just a little more sunshine and she will be outside, her tiny silken form trying to keep up with the ever-changing ideas that enter her exquisite head. In true cat tradition she loves to roll in my puny catmint but otherwise is well behaved among the flowers.

The heavy branches of a *Prunus serrulata* 'Schimidsu Sakura' form an arch over our cottage entrance. They are laden with dangling bunches of green buds and at any moment the semi-double white flowers will emerge, filling the air around the door with their fragrance. An enveloping blanket of *Clematis montana* covers our porch. Tumbling in falls of bud-laden streamers, it has obscured all windows in its path and is now marching resolutely over the top of a nearby lilac tree. Soon its flowers will open and the front of the cottage will be covered in a veil of vanilla-scented blossoms.

Crystalized flowers and leaves make beautiful decorations for cakes, and even puddings and ice-cream. Sweet Cicely (top right) and mint leaves are particularly delicious when crystalized. The other plants featured here are white forget-me-not, alpine strawberry, parsley, daisies, and violets.

The garden is becoming greener each day and I notice that the interesting old-fashioned English vernal primroses are coming out. Jack-in-the-green, hose-in-hose, gallygaskins, Jackanapes, Jackanapes-on-horseback; what enchanting names these old Elizabethan primroses have. Many diffuse sweet perfume that varies from plant to plant – some even smell of honeysuckle. Facing northeast and having a rich acid soil, our garden is a paradise for most members of the primula family. Over the years I have grown, and often hand-pollinated, many of the interesting mutant primroses. James Thomson wrote:

> *– where Beauty plays*
> *Her idle Freaks: from family diffus'd*
> *To Family, as flies the Father-Dust,*
> *The varied colours run.*

26

*Dainty lady's smock,
bluebells, green-
centered hellebores
and white-edged lilac
'Sensation' look even
daintier when
contrasted with clove-
studded pomanders.*

CAULDRON OF SPRING POTPOURRI

*T*HE bulk of this mix is pale mauve statice flowers which merge beautifully with all the other purple blossoms incorporated into the potpourri. Bluebells press well, but they are far lovelier either dried in silica gel or hung upside down in a warm spot. They deepen in colour and contract, but their exquisite form is retained. Hellebores, double mayflowers and lilac also press well, but dry even better in silica gel. These are all evocative spring flowers and I have made them into the focal point of this spring potpourri.

The bluebells and double lady's smock are tied into bunches, simply because that is how I always visualize them.

For contrast of texture and perfume, add some sharp lemon pomanders, a few dried peel flowers and a bunch of giant cinnamon sticks. To make the citrus peel flowers, cut the fruit in half, squeeze out all the juice and remove any remaining flesh. Snip the remaining "cups" of peel in four places, not quite severing the sections at the base. Round off the corners of each section and then dry them very slowly in a lukewarm oven. Thick-skinned lemons are particularly attractive when dried in this way.

Perfume this spring potpourri with syringa, lavender and lemon oil, or any similar essential flower oil. The tangy smell of the lemon flowers and pomanders can be quite strong.

Mix all the following dry ingredients together thoroughly, add the essential oils and store for six weeks in an airtight container, shaking daily, before using.

Bluebells, lady's smock, lilac and hellebore flowers to decorate the top of the potpourri.

1 quart mauve statice flowers

2 oz lavender

1 oz orris root powder

1 tsp ground allspice

6 dried lemon-peel flowers

4 lemon pomanders

6 drops syringa oil

4 drops lavender oil

The prettiness of the flowers in this old cauldron contrasts well with the thick black iron of the pot.

The wild area of the garden reflects the tropical steamy atmosphere of the river banks and every year it runs totally out of control. Sunlight filtering through the giant gunnera leaves floods the wilderness with green light.

And what beautiful and powerful words they are, describing so eloquently the behavior of my promiscuous primroses! With an obsessive interest I have watched the effect of the "Father's-Dust" (pollen) on my plants and, as spring after spring has passed, so the primroses have proliferated. The pollen has blown far and wide begetting ever-changing colors, ruffles, streaking, doubling-up, lacing and all the odd things that primroses get up to. The bees also transport the pollen even farther afield than the wind could carry it and each spring I search for the unusual flowers which appear in the surrounding fields, in the lane opposite the cottage, and in the nooks and crannies of the garden. Sadly, over the last few years they have not been quite so abundant as primroses need a lot of attention and I have very little time. They must have a yearly feed of well-rotted farmyard manure, be divided at least every second year and, if possible, moved to a completely new site every four or five years. As for culinary matters, all primroses crystalize beautifully and I like to decorate creamy-topped puddings with them – they add a delicious something.

The dainty, fernlike foliage of the "Threepenny-Bit" rose (*Rosa farreri persetosa*) is coming out and must be pressed before it coarsens. Carpets of bright pink dog violets are spreading over the terrace and wherever they can gain a foothold in the flower borders. Like quite a few other plants, dog violets really are gypsies, for after a couple of years they will up and move house, leaving not a plant behind, only to reappear in profusion elsewhere. Yellow, apricot, white, mauve and purple violets are also out in bloom which are beautiful when crystalized. They also press well as whole specimens, their hairlike roots, fragile flowers and familiar leaves looking most appealing lightly glued to a rough-textured, card.

The blackthorn is not yet out, but the masses of tiny flower buds that bedeck the bare twigs are fascinating for they resemble minuscule green hot cross buns, each with a perfect white cross on top. The daffodils are out in profusion, though. Mine are sturdy old-fashioned, slightly over-dressed, varieties and they spread in trembling yellow crowds across the lawns. When the sun comes out, and if there is some warmth in it, I like to sit among them. Their fragrance is faint and evasive, rather like that of the primrose; a perfume of childhood like ivy leaves, white violets, elder wood and wild strawberries.

COLLAGE OF A VASE OF FLOWERS

*I*N this collage, I have arranged a jumble of pressed and dried spring flowers above a green seaweed-decorated vase. I enjoy mixing dried three-dimensional blossoms with their pressed counterparts; the overall effect is fascinating and infinitely more pleasing than a flat surface, particularly in an arrangement such as this one.

This collage has been photographed in the very wildest area of the garden where the cow parsley towers 7 feet into the air before collapsing in great lacy bundles.

Hellebores and double and single kingcups dry extremely well in silica gel, as do bergenias and anemones. The checkered bells of the fritillaria are too rounded to be dried and used in a collage such as this one, so newly opened bells must be carefully pressed.

Fern fronds can be pressed, but if gluing them over the three-dimensional flowers only attach them at the base of the stalk, tucking each stalk neatly behind a flower, and then again at about 1½ inches from the tip. In this way the pretty dainty foliage falls quite freely.

For the vase, cut the required shape from stiff card stock, give it a wash of forest green, cover it with skeletonized leaves and decorate it with pressed seaweeds. Using the usual rubber cement, secure it onto a sheet of handmade paper before arranging the blossoms and ferns above it.

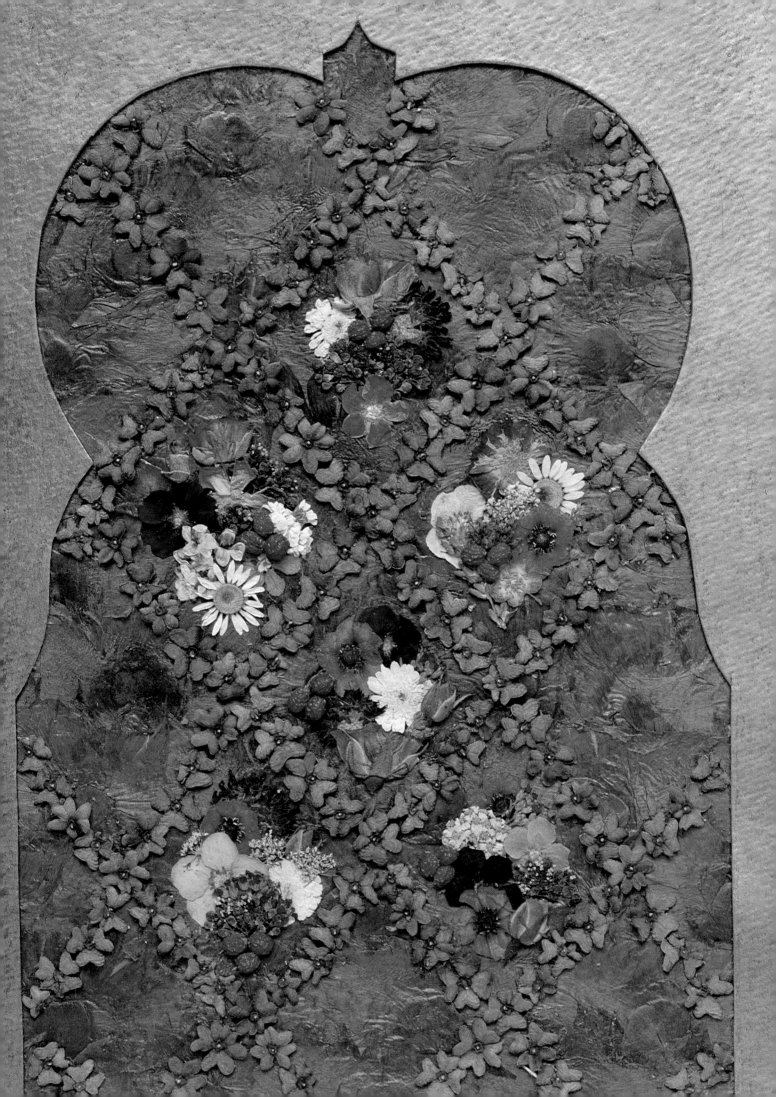

ISLAMIC-STYLE PRESSED FLOWER PICTURES

PREVIOUS PAGE
I have always been fascinated by the rich opulent colors in Islamic art; the scintillating royal blue, purple, and sea and emerald greens are so rich. Equally, the exquisite patterns and colors of Islamic tiles, the silks and satins of Turkish, ancient Persian and Arabian textiles, and the intricate ivory, jade and crystal jewelery are quite beautiful.

OR these pictures, I wanted to use some of the beautiful Islamic colors and shapes reminiscent of the Middle East. The end results are two stylized gardens seen through the filigree of a screen, bordered by Moorish arches.

The arches are cut from card and gold leaf applied to add to the depth and splendor. Decorate the background card before attaching the arches. To ensure sufficient background is covered, use the arches as a template and mark where the arches will fall on the card.

The backgrounds for the collages are made from tissue-paper, thin tropical seedpods, bought from a herb importer. As they are naturally pale cream, carefully dye some emerald green and others royal blue using acrylic dye. With a cool iron, press them dry to ensure that they remain flat.

Using rubber cement, attach the seedpods to the card rectangles putting the royal blue pods on one sheet and the emerald green ones on the other. You need only cover the area a little beyond the guideline of the Moorish arch previously drawn on the card.

The blue picture is a mass of blossoms and foliage partially obscuring a night sky. Pretty blue, cream, pale green and pinkish brown flowers, together with some moss are glued in place to create a thickly textured group, roughly positioned in the center of the picture. After gluing a gilded arch in place, add some perpendicular columns of rosebuds and spindle berries.

The green picture is more reminiscent of an embroidery than a garden, although the posies of flowers evoke a blossoming wilderness. For this picture, glue the gilded arch in place before decorating the centerpiece. Textured spindle berries are glued along guidelines to create the latticework. Other small and interesting botanicals such as star anise, cloves and allspice are equally appropriate. Posies of flowers and berries are arranged within the middle lattices, leaving the outer edges unadorned in order to emphasise the central richness of the picture.

The great yellow spathes of the skunk cabbage are out around the pond, and their fetid smell mixes with that of the water hawthorn creating a surprisingly pleasant bouquet. The jute-colored flowers of the woodrush are in bloom, too. These sparse, brown, mop-heads of grass flowers are indispensable both dried and pressed. When pressed they can be used as ecru lacy edgings, and when dried they add a light and misty touch to any arrangement. The ribbed leaves of the hostas are unfurling, as are the woolly fern fronds uncurling. Pink water blinks have selfseeded like mustard and cress and the white variety is already in bloom. The hundreds of bog primulas are fattening like lusty cabbages and the flower buds are showing deep within the plants. Giant grasses are pushing their green, yellow, white and even fiery red shoots through the earth. Pretty, tufted, meadowsweet leaves are already 6 inches high and beautiful crosiers of comfrey flowers are just waiting for the sunshine to open their delicate pastel bells. The tightly-packed, crumpled leaves of the ornamental rhubarbs are breaking away from their tissue paper sheaths, and all my lovely *Fritillaria meleagris*, in shades of purple, to gray, to green, to white, are just beginning to heave themselves off the ground. Each year, I think they have been trampled on because of their rather odd mode of growth, but of course they have not; they just happen to crawl out of the earth rather than push nose first. White and pink *Dicentra spectabilis* are out, as are the first kingcups and early cultivated buttercups. Spring is gathering pace in my garden and the blackbird is perched high, his liquid song echoing through the garden.

There are lots of flowers to press and dry now, not forgetting buds and newly opened leaves. Violets, kingcups, periwinkles, grape hyacinths, euphorbias, dandelions, pulmonarias, daffodils and anything that really that takes your fancy. Daffodils dry very well in silica gel. Blackthorn twigs, adorned with their little round buds, can be pressed under strong pressure. Just one spray decorating a pale gray-washed card looks like a fragile Oriental watercolor.

The warm light of a setting sun burnishes the west-facing branches of the Monterey pines with gold, and even the dead storm-tossed boughs have a moment of glory. Alone in a silver-dusted, aquamarine sky a creamy moon displays her mountains. The last humble bumblebee drones its way home and the first pipistrelle bat appears from nowhere.

Along the lane I can smell the wild garlic and ransoms, their white flowers glistening in the faded light. The gorse blossom has thickened, strengthening its coconut fragrance which drifts around and about. Soft, white dandelion clocks wait for their seeds to be carried away on the air and the last of the bleached celandines tightly closes her petals. A dew falls on my earthly paradise and the birds of the valley gloriously sing their vespers. The moon glows golden in the darkening sky and one tiny star has seeded alongside her. A gentle breeze turns icy, another star appears, and I can smell frost in the air. Suddenly the day has ended for the birds and, within a minute, their evening song – just as beautiful as their dawn chorus – has ended too. I meander back to my garden where all the white flowers hang stalkless in the twilight. The dew has stirred the toads and they are lolloping in and out of the flower borders and along the winding paths of the wild garden. Walking beneath the overhanging boughs of the hawthorns, I disturb large roosting birds and their desperate exit from the tangled branches takes me by surprise and tightens my chest with fear. Struggling to gain height, their wings clap and thrash and suddenly my familiar garden has become hostile, and I hurry toward the cottage feeling that all the hobgoblins of childhood are after me.

Blue-, pink- and whitebells grow in a meandering river of blossom across the lawn and into the woodland flower borders.

Blackthorn flowers late in our valley but now the leafless branches have been sifted with fluffy-stamened white blossoms and the boughs of the wild cherry too are hung with their ephemeral pale flowers. The grass paths and lawns have become snowy rivers of daisies and when the sun shines I stop to search for the pink-tipped flowers, less common than the all-white daisy. They were perhaps more abundant when Lord Tennyson wrote:

> *I know the way she went*
> *Home with her maiden posy,*
> *For her feet have touched the meadows*
> *And left the daisies rosy.*

Or at least that is what I like to read into these lines. Pink-tipped or white they are pretty when pressed and exquisite when crystalized.

Sweet woodruff is flowering in and around the plants of the shady areas, and the blossoms are as white as my father's shirts that blew on the clothesline in my mother's garden. Pure white flowers are few and far between, but I have found a few: white honesty flowers are of the purest white, as are white daisies of every variety, dame's violet, libertia, white forget-me-nots and white mallow.

SKELETONIZED COLLAGE

*T*HIS large, leaf-shaped collage, made from five skeletonized magnolia leaves and decorated with fragile pressed ferns is a far cry from my usual work. Here is something visually quite simple and refreshing.

The basis of this collage is skeletonized leaves whose structure is reminiscent of the wings of a lacewing fly. It is decorated with a few fronds of maidenhair fern.

There is an appealing simplicity to this soothing and cool picture.

On the edges of our lane the bramble's needle has been threaded and her leaf-adorned twine has been looped and stitched among the bluebells, campions, stitchwort, violets and ferns and even woven through the sheaves of honeysuckle. Over the moorland and fields, the skylark trills and sings her heart out and this morning a first swallow, a second and then a third, twisted and looped over the barn. I opened all the dilapidated doors in a gesture of welcome and they will remain open all the summer.

Luscious spring is burgeoning and I can enjoy all the weeds of the hedgerow and their smell. The spring birds, willow warbler and swallow are with us, white clouds race over a forget-me-not-blue sky, our garden is lush with newborn beauty and there are butterflies everywhere. The orange-tip butterfly lays her eggs on lady's-smock and dame's violet, both of which grow in profusion in the garden, so sunny days see this butterfly fluttering around one of my favorite spring flowers, the double lady's smock. Very occasionally found in the wild, this flower is a treasure in a cottage garden, being of the purest pale mauve color, and occasionally white, with tightly-packed double flowers that decorate thin and elegant 6-inch stems. It has all the delicate beauty of spring and I grow my plants in gauzy lavender drifts. To increase this precious little plant, nip off a basal leaf and push the lower quarter of the leaf into any fairly moist soil where it will invariably root and flower the following year. As it is double, it does not, as is the usual rule, produce any seeds.

I love to be in the garden in the half light of early morning and dusk.

> *When the fast ushering star of morning comes*
> *O'eriding the grey hills with golden scarf;*
> *Or when the cowled and dusky-sandaled Eve,*
> *In mourning weeds, from out the Western gates,*
> *Departs with silent pace!*

LONGFELLOW

Here in Cornwall strong winds and frequent gales shape our landscape and our gardens, but in the twilight moments, a tranquility often descends upon our "little land". I think almost all Cornish gardeners love these moments and we are all prone to meandering around our gardens in the half light, taking advantage of a pause for breath by the capricious weather. How well I know my garden in faded light and in shades of gray and silver.

I love the giant 8 foot fronds of the New Zealand tree fern. These dried leaves look beautiful as an outdoor arrangement. I have crammed them into a very old and rusty milkchurn.

This arrangement of grasses has been photographed in my potting shed; their beauty has been enhanced by the green-washed light flooding in through the doorway.

ARRANGEMENT OF SPRING GRASSES IN A TIN HAT BOX

I GATHERED this assortment of spring grasses during a meander down our lane. They are all lovers of damp, acid soil and they look particularly beautiful jumbled together and crammed into an old hat box.

⁓ There is no need to arrange grasses in water for they will not wilt. Instead, they gradually dry in the pretty pendulous form that they have in this arrangement.

⁓ As the grasses slowly dessicate it may be necessary to add a few more sprays, but fresh or dry, they will always have the elegant daintiness that only grasses possess.

It is daybreak in our late spring garden, but in a sapphire sky, suffused with violet and cyclamen, the brightest sickle moon still hangs over the earth. The grass of the upper lawns is gray with dew, and in their air hangs the incense of all the perfumes of the night. Every bird that ever was seems to be singing and for a moment I am overwhelmed by the volume of their song. Above all it is the pure liquid beauty of the blackbird's music that seduces my ears and I can hear his song echoed by his companions along the lane and across the fields. A woodpecker hammers in the distance and the first cockerel begins to crow.

Frost coats the bracken and bluebells along the banks of the river, but the taller mints under the willows are only felted with dew. The eastern horizon is illuminated apricot by impending dawn, while in the west, the sky is still night veiled. I can just distinguish the color green. Slowly a folded and creased veil of smoky cloud drifts over the earliest blue sky and I can see the blue of the bluebells and yellow of kingcups. The campions, herb Robert and bog primulas gradually emerge in all their pinks and finally even the dark red flowers become visible. And with the arrival of early light the birdsong diminishes to chatters and tweets.

The ephemeral veiling has left the sky, the moon is paling and the frost is melting, running to the tips of the leaves and hanging in droplets that are not quite sparkling. Beneath the top wall of the opposite field lie a long straggly ribbon of cows, huffing and puffing and chewing their cud. Slowly the first cow heaves herself onto her feet, and after gazing for a moment at the early morning, starts to crop the lush grass. A second animal gets to her feet, but as if still entranced by night, just gazes languidly at nothing. The moon has gone and a pearled light glistens on spring's first tented cobwebs. Two doves coo in the sycamores behind the cottage; tiny birds squabble in the blackthorns; the woodpecker starts to hammer quite earnestly, and as I look across the valley, the cows are all up and about their business of eating. The sky is now as clear as only a very early sky can become and I am suddenly aware of how cold I am. The cottage welcomes me with the warmth of the kitchen stove and Ebony, who is sitting in the warming oven, looks at me as if I'm quite mad to have been out in the garden at such as unearthly hour.

A meandering river of bluebells flows from the top of the garden, across the upper lawns and then filters into the woodland beds in a haze of blue.

BOTANICAL HERB PICTURE

*T*HE historical significance and lore surrounding flowers and herbs is quite absorbing and I believe that an important aspect of gardening, often neglected, is an understanding as to how our past has been shaped by the botanical world. To learn a little of the history of a plant totally changes the attitude that one may have toward it.

There is no artistry in a collage such as this and yet the end result is decorative and refined.

⤔ This botanical collage is created on a piece of crackled white-painted wood, and its effect is reminiscent of a page from an old herbal, or perhaps a poster from an apothecary's premises.

⤔ Annotate all the plants, using their old-fashioned names and use strips of torn, handmade paper for the labels. It might also be fun to add an old herbal rhyme, again written on torn-edged handmade paper.

⤔ Use rubber cement to stick both the botanicals and the paper onto the wood. It does not matter if the paper wrinkles when glued in place, as this adds to the character of the collage.

⤔ Finally, for protection, evenly spray the collage with a coat of matte polyurethane varnish.

A few exquisite pinkbells and whitebells are scattered here and there among the bluebells. Warm sun has released their spicy perfume, and as I walk among them I am aware of an enveloping fragrant humidity. Hovering around the blossoms, velvety fox-red and black, gray and yellow, and dark brown bumblebees, honeybees and flies in profusion, whine and buzz their way into the striped pale and dark blue bells. On the steep banks of the Cornish lanes, bluebells tangle with an enveloping flood of lacy cow parsley, erect pink campions and spires of shivering rusty sorrel. The perfume trapped within the lanes is overwhelming and makes me sneeze, for the cinnamon fragrance of the bluebells is diluted by the slightly musty smell of the cow parsley. In the dappled sunlight of woodland, the bluebells bloom in supreme glory, for this is their true home. There is nothing more beautiful than an English bluebell wood.

In my own garden, orchids are establishing themselves among the bluebells. The orchids must have been there since time immemorial, but having been cropped by generations of cattle they remained hidden underground. Now, however, they are appearing all over the place. What a bonus! Cow parsley is out in our wild garden, sending 7-foot branched stalks into the skies only to collapse, obscuring paths and soaking the legs and feet of those who admire it. In the more cultivated areas of the garden I grow pretty pale-mauve cow parsley and a precious salmon-pink one too. I plant the wildling here, there and everywhere, for I love the softening effect that the umbels of white lace have on more formal plantings. Forget-me-nots are billowing around everything; the white ones speckling the dusk garden with their tiny flowers.

Sunlight filtering through the giant gunnera leaves floods the wilderness with green light. The huge tasseled cones of the flowers are quite alien in the English landscape, but they add to the exotic atmosphere.

As the leaves on the trees thicken, so the garden has become more sheltered. When the sun shines, the damp earth steams and I can almost hear the plants squeak as they grow. Spring is beginning to run away with herself and the chaos of blossom and new growth far exceeds that of gardens at a lower altitude. Today I have heard the cuckoo for the first time; there will be no shortage of host nests and adoptive parents for the garden is heaving with birds and wildlife in general. Already the growth is so lush that vision is restricted to a few yards. Tall comfreys, masses of cultivated buttercups, angelica, Siberian and flag iris, hundreds of blue and white Jacob's ladder and a multitude of other plants flop over the wide grass paths. Towering skyward, twice the average height, they obscure vision around corners and through borders.

44

At the turn of the century our miner's cottages were inhabited by the local butcher and the barns were used to slaughter the animals. For forty years all the blood and bones were dumped into what is now our two-acre garden. Whenever a spade is put into the soil, large, perfect teeth and crumbling bones are uncovered. Of course, this has immensely enriched the soil, turning it into a friable, acid loam. Water running off the fields above the cottage, through the garden and into the river, together with frequent and saturating mists, all add to the Asiatic conditions of the lower garden that runs level with the small river. All the beautiful candelabra primulas proliferate in their thousands; deciduous azaleas perfume the air and now that the garden has become so sheltered, the rhododendrons are thriving. Huge mounds of hostas, ferns, rhubarb, blue, yellow and red Himalayan poppies, grasses, bamboos, rushes, alliums, orchids and giant mints, nearly all lovers of the Himalayan slopes, manifest their presence in late spring. But in spite of all the pageantry of these plants in the lower flower beds, our garden remains a cottage garden and elsewhere spring turns to summer more gently. It will always be the old-fashioned plants and many of the wild flowers that occupy the special niche in my heart.

Our azure stream of bluebells has now faded into a pale ribbon of 'graybells', 'the moonlight-colored may' flower is in bloom and all the white blossoms of spring-turning-to-summer are out. Late cow parsley, white Jacob's ladder and dame's violet, dog daisies, elder flowers and pear blossom, white lilac and precious white ragged robins and herb Robert are all pale flowers of late spring and early summer. Fragile spring retreats in a hush of white, knowing that her beauty will remain unsurpassed. I am left just a little sad, for no other season can diffuse such delight within me. But there is all the glorious pomp of summer to come and I love that too.

> No more shall violets linger in the dell,
> Or purple orchis variegate the plain,
> Till spring shall call forth every bell,
> And dress with humid hands,
>   her wreaths again.

CHARLOTTE SMITH

For striped collages, all sorts of different colored backgrounds can enhance rows of flowers. Shrivelled berries and tiny seedheads come into their own, as do small leaves and even mung beans. For this collage there is a formality of structure, reminiscent of a sampler, derived from my lifelong interest in textiles.

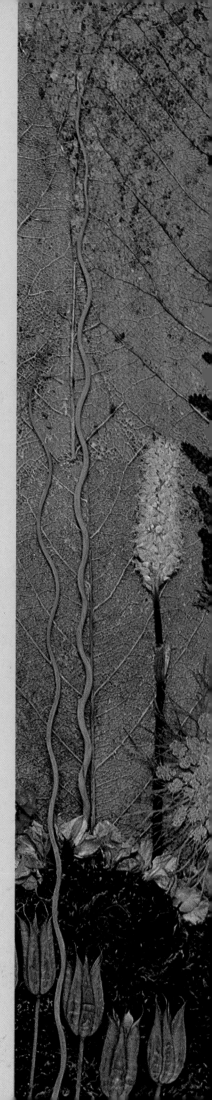

PART TWO

SUMMER

'... in gusts of scented wind

Swirling out bloom till all the air is

blind

With rosy foam and pelting blossom

and mists

Of driving vermeil-rain;'

GERARD MANLEY HOPKINS

Summer has arrived with the rose-stained petals of winnowed hawthorn. They dust the hedgerows in faded pink flakes and their sickly incense no longer pervades the air beneath the tangled branches. Already, green-budded spires of pennywort and foxglove are pushing through wreaths of lady's bedstraw and ivy, posies of blue sheep's bit scabious and bunches of the new silky flower heads of hedgerow grasses. The river is choked with water hemlock, and feathered mounds of joe-pye weed and ferns obscure the banks. The white butterflies of early summer have arrived and so have tiny midges, dragon- and damsel-flies, more bees, and the garden and willow warblers. Spring's last flowers are withdrawing and I know that early summer is gathering strength for the verdant chaos that is to come.

> I sing of Brooks, of Blossoms, Birds and Bowers:
> Of April, May, of June, and July-Flowers . . .
> I sing of Dews, of Rains, and piece by piece
> Of Balm, of Oil, of Spice, and Amber-Greece.

In Robert Herrick's words the very essence of the fragrant disorder of our summer garden is captured.

Pale drifts of green-white, milky-blue and white columbines are flowering among the sweet Cicely, bergamot, sage, artemesias, horehound and French sorrel of the herb borders. The exquisite flowers hang like porcelain lanterns and light the shade beneath the canopy of crab apple. In the shady areas of the lower garden, the Hensol harebell nods her aristocratic wedgewood-blue head. Given a chance she will cross with any other columbine and I love the whole tribe. The *Buddleia globosa* is now fully out and the spongy flower balls are as orange as an orange. Walking beneath the tree is like spreading honey on toast, for the sweet fragrance overwhelms the olfactory nerves. Bury your nose in *Buddleia globosa* flowers and they become a whole pot of honey! The shrubby *Euphorbia melifera* is also honey-scented, and the perfume can be quite alarming if you are not familiar with it.

The double shocking-pink wild campion is flowering but, as always, has only produced a couple of flowers – just to remind me of her existence. Astrantias, or Hattie's pincushion, as is the appropriate country name for them, love this garden and thrive in a wide variety. In particular, their papery blossoms vary immensely.

It may come as a surprise, but this photograph is of our pond. The water is only visible during the winter months for the rapid growth rate of the plants in the warm, nitrogen-enriched water covers the entire surface of the pond by early summer. Arum lilies grow in abundance as do water hawthorn and water plantain.

TWIGGY CUPBOARD

From the moment I first saw this twig cupboard I loved it. I could just visualize it in our garden, for I can see no reason why pretty, durable wooden furniture should not embellish and enhance the outside of any house. It is now possible to buy delightful imported furniture, and because much of it is wood it is eminently suitable for the garden. This twig cupboard, in the style of Appalachian furniture, looks quite beautiful nestled against the front of the cottage.

Ivies trail around treasures dug up in the garden. Old stout bottles, ink wells and a small decorated washbowl have found a home in this quaint cupboard.

The cupboard is filled with pots of ivies, pansies, and mind-your-own-business.

In time, the ivy will overwhelm the cupboard and then it will be time to start all over again with a completely different selection of plants.

The flamboyance of early summer is over, and the borders are displaying taller mid-summer flowers in more gentle hues. Gray-leaved giant mints and lemon-yellow Lysimachia ciliata *love the damp, almost soggy soil. A pretty white-veined form of* Geranium pratense *is exuberant in her growth and will continue flowering well into late summer.*

I have huge shaggy white ones whose petals are green tipped and spoon shaped, green maturing to pink ones, small dark red ones, unadorned white ones and, of course, the variegated leaf variety. They all press and dry extremely well. The herbaceous *Clematis durandii* is also flowering and what a jewel it is. The nodding indigo-violet, cream-stamened flowers are unique in their form and the thick petals (or to be botanically accurate calyx, for they have no true petals) twist as they mature, giving the flower a supreme Oriental elegance. Tall fluffy-headed thalictrums are out in pale lilac and in white, and they have seeded around among the Hensol harebells, whose leaves are almost identical to those of the thalictrums. Enormous clumps of creamy white and every shade of blue and purple *Iris sibirica* are opening their long pointed buds. I am an ardent collector of the lovely herbaceous geraniums which are flopping around in their usual profusion. I also grow many large ornamental grasses one of my favourites being *Stipa gigantea*, a member of the oat family.

The later flowering Asiatic primulas are now coming out and the orange-scarlet spires of *Primula* 'Inverewe' dazzle the eye. Growing happily, and almost as flamboyantly, with this outstanding hybrid are apricot, tangerine, shocking-pink, yellow, burnt-orange and carmine candelabra primulas. I am beguiled by this witchery of clashing colors reminiscent of Mexican embroideries. Waving around among these hot-headed primulas is the much coveted *Ranunculus ledebourii*. The globe-shaped flowers are the color of the yolk of a brown egg, and they are filled with a seething mass of orange stamens. They look beautiful mixed with my fiery señoritas. A small and very double form of the wild buttercup lives with this extrovert throng, and you can almost hear her saying "What a good girl am I" when she sees all the progeny of her wild companions, for they seed around in their thousands, but the little buttercup, being fully double, will never seed at all.

This pretty garland of wild and cottage garden flowers reflects the simplicity and tradition of a country wedding. The poetry also evokes the delights of such an occasion. I felt quite a sense of occasion as I arranged love-in-a-mist, comfrey bells, maidenhair fern and roses on a background of glistening Cornish moss.

Epithalamium —
The pink-turned-blue forget-me-not
   With no stalks on its leaves;
The sun-gold ladies bedstraw
   (No sting nor prickle leaves);
Love-in-a-mist sky-blue and white,
   Soft maiden-hair and comfrey —
These will delight my girl tonight
   With heartsease in the country.

Francis Warner 1983

56

PREVIOUS PAGE
Whenever I hang my herbs to dry over the kitchen stove I am reminded of just how lovely they look and never want to take them down. The herbs dry extremely quickly in our warm kitchen. A golden rule when drying all botanicals is to ensure that the process is speedy, for they will then retain most of their colour and perfume. I love the old traditional blue and white china and have collected it for years.

I can't recall a year when the angelica has been lovelier and my plants have grown into enormous 8-foot succulent giants. I love these old and very holy biennials. The textured, apple-green umbels are cool and tightly packed with small knobbly flowers, and I dry them, together with the fragrant leaves and roots, for use in potpourris. Being the most holy plant in the garden, as all the old herbals will inform you, I find it very amusing that vervain, the most magical plant, should seed itself beside such an angel. Vervain is as squinty as *Angelica archangelica* is grand and I love the incongruity of the partnership. I hope everyone else does for I enthusiastically point them out to all and sundry.

Mimulus is now blooming all over the place, and it is a plant partial to seeding in extraordinary situations. One year all the paths of the low-lying area of the garden became dazzling yellow monkey-flower pools. I would not allow anyone to mow them for weeks which I suppose reflects my unconventional style of gardening. But I love nature's largesse and so, when the gutters of the barn supported a wonderful colony of red-spotted mimulus, that too was allowed to remain. In addition to the wild monkey flower I grow orange *Mimulus auranticus*, red *Mimulus cardinalis* and mauve *Mimulus ringens*. I even have a hose-in-hose variety. *Mimulus moschatus*, the musk flower of cottage gardens, used to be grown for its perfume. But in 1913, and almost overnight, all *Mimulus moschatus* throughout the world reverted to their hairless form and also lost their rich perfume that was similar to that of the musk mallow, musk storksbill and musk thistle. To my knowledge no one has yet discovered the cause of this most strange phenomenon.

I am fascinated by all wild plants that show some deviation from the norm and have assembled quite a collection. Of course, they are coveted by many gardeners and AE Bowles had a corner of his garden, somewhat appropriately named "The Lunatic Asylum", where he grew as many of nature's mistakes as he could lay his hands on. In fact, he writes so wittily and eloquently of them that he must have titillated the imagination of many a gardener, as indeed he has mine. I have a mild affection for both the contorted willow and hazel, but would never be without my clump of contorted rush. The leaves are crimped to a corkscrew perfection and are the envy of all flower arrangers. They press beautifully and always arouse attention when used as a strong vertical point of interest in a collage.

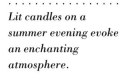

Lit candles on a summer evening evoke an enchanting atmosphere.

FLOWERY CANDLES

*N*othing could be prettier than the soft honeyed light of flower-adorned candles on a still summer evening. They are most elegant when decorated with very delicate pressed flowers and leaves.

 The beautiful veining on many petals is exquisitely highlighted when coated with translucent wax and surrounded by the glow of the burning wick.

The Thicker botanicals can only be used with fire-lit illumination as ornamentation on a wax bowl with a candle inside it. Any fire hazard is then obviated because the source of light remains undecorated. Only thin pressed botanicals should be used as decoration on candles, and these should never be left burning unattended.

The Great care must be taken when making or decorating candles: because wax is highly inflammable, it should always be melted in a double-boiler-type pan and removed from the heat source before use. The pressed decorations are then lightly held in place on the candle and brushed with melted wax.

INDIAN PATCHWORK COLLAGE

The freestyle, stylized and geometric Indian embroideries offer inspiration, and a patchwork of scraps reflecting these styles is a cornucopia of ideas.

I have always been fascinated by Indian textiles. I love the hand-dyed cotton fabrics, the prolific embroidery and the unusual use of color. The old faded and threadbare embroideries are even more fascinating, emanating a spirit from the past. I find their muted colors and remnants of stitchery quite captivating. I gathered notions for my collage from two cushions, both made from odd snippets of varied embroideries. As in the cushions, there is no order in my design other than the use of sections that are either square or rectangular.

Pencil the design on the background card and assemble a variety of dried and pressed petals, flower heads, leaves and whole spices. I wanted to combine faded mauve with purple, royal blue with tangerine, and turquoise with pink, at the same time introducing jade and emerald green, red and brown. These colors are prolific in Indian textiles and the muted colors of botanicals are very similar to the faded and inspirational embroidery silks.

To surprise and charm the eye, introduce flashes of vivid acrylic colors and perhaps a little white or pale yellow.

In all collages, texture is as important as color and mixing rough shriveled petals with smooth leaves, three-dimensional knobbly flowers with flat sprays and even hard brown whole spices with fragile blossoms adds a greater depth to a design. There is infinite contrast of texture in embroidery, for each stitch has a different surface, and fabrics can offer enormous inspiration.

The background to the ornamentation consists of rectangles of red rose and blue larkspur petals, lavender and anaphalis flowers and whole allspice berries. These sections give the collage its patchwork feel. Divide the patches by formal rows of flowers and decorate.

SUMMER ROSE POTPOURRI

The upturned top of an old wickerwork table holds a wonderful display of dried old roses. Almost every pink and red rose in the garden has been included and even the single rugosa roses have dried well. Mixed with the whole roses are dark red dried petals gathered from the deliciously scented rose 'Roseraie de l'Hay'.

To make a finely scented summer potpourri, mix the dried roses with lavender and spices. This is probably the most traditional of all potpourris and it remains fragrant for a very long time.

When the perfume fades, just mix a few drops of the essential oils listed below with some ground cloves and add the mixture to the roses, mixing them thoroughly.

Mix together all the following dry ingredients, add the essential oils and store for six weeks in an airtight container, shaking daily, before using.

1 quart dried roses and petals
2 oz lavender
1 oz orris root powder (or fine-ground gum benzoin)
2 tsp ground cloves
½ tsp allspice
½ tsp grated nutmeg
dried rind of a lemon
6 drops rose oil
2 drops lavender oil

The table is standing on the herb path and is surrounded by the summer's earliest hydrangeas and all sorts of aromatic artemesias, including lad's love who should always be tweaked when passed.

I love the green-rinsed light of the wild steamy areas of the garden. Here everything grows in lush abandon and ferns, water hemlock, sedges and the overhanging branches all tangle one with the other, weaving the esoteric atmosphere of a sheltered Cornish valley.

The blotched-leaved hawkweed attracts a lot of comment too, and I am surprised that it is not more widely grown. I was amazed and delighted to see the small, black-bespattered leaves growing on the hillsides of southwest France; obviously it is so common as to have become almost a variety. The plantains are also great deviators and I grow the beetroot-leaved and the tufted varieties. The wild wood sage can appear with tightly goffered edges to its leaves as can some of the mints, and they are all quite rampant in our damp soil. Crested ferns are well worth growing and in my garden the hart's-tongue fern frequently appears with forked and tufted leaves.

Just as I have great affection for all these oddities so, too, do I love all the white-blossomed forms of the wild flowers. Dwarf and tall varieties of white herb Robert seed themselves around the entire garden; white betony and white field scabious are cool and elegant; white dog violets, sheep's bit scabious, white thyme and marjoram are charming, and the pale greeny white flowers of the water avens captivate everyone. There is also the white rosebay willow herb, which grows in invasive drifts in the lower garden. It took me years to acquire it and even after many seasons in the garden it can still fill me with delight and pride. But closest to my heart are the infinitely delicately frayed flowers of the white ragged robin. A few years ago I was given a precious two plants and I have found that its fragile appearance does not belie its constitution, for each year it is tardy in blooming and has not increased in size or seeded around. I take great care of it and always make a point of showing it to visitors to the garden.

In the woodland area, a thin canopy of new leaves allows dappled sunlight to fall on a gathering wilderness of campions, pale and dark blue alkanet (whose roots release a red dye that was used to color rose perfume pink), Pyrenean valerian, dame's violet, comfreys and ferns in variety, white and blue Jacob's ladder, wild sorrel, anthericums and any other plants that are strong enough to survive the flamboyant growth of their neighbors. When a breeze stirs the overhead leaves,

> *Sunlight gathers its rays*
> *In sheaves, which the wind unweaves*
> *And then reweaves – the wind*
> *That puffs a smell of grass*
> *Through the heat-heavy, trembling*
> *Summer pool of air.*
>
> ASJ TESSIMOND

I love this early summer woodland where the shade pales the campions and sorrel and the clove-like fragrance of the night-scented dame's violet lingers in the half light. The river hurries over mossy granite bedrock and ancient ivied willows bridge the peaty water. As the wood becomes wilder so the native trees of the valley are to be found and introduced plants give way to creeping Jenny, common meadow rue, wild monkshood, bog willow herb, wood sorrel, yellow pimpernel, sedges, water mint, figwort, mare's tail, lesser spearwort and even the diminutive ivy-leaved bellflower.

There is now the beginnings of a cornucopia of flowers and leaves to press and dry. Sorrel, Jacob's ladder, deutzia, philadelphus, contorted rush spikes, lady's mantle, ferns and fresh new herb foliage can be gathered. And lilac –

> *Who thought of the Lilac?*
> *'I' the Dew said*
> *'I made up the Lilac*
> *out of my head.'*

Well, the dew was infinitely clever when she made up lilac 'Sensation' for that is what the purple white-edged blossoms are. It is the only lilac that presses really well and it should have just the lightest pressure applied during the drying process. The result is wonderful; textured cones of deep violet white-bordered flowers that will add an unsurpassed luxuriance to any collage. These blossoms also dry well in silica gel.

64

In the garden, total chaos manifests itself almost overnight. Walking toward the lower flower borders, pushing my way between plants and ducking overhanging branches, I realize that law and order has been totally abandoned, and that our two acres has become a wild and tangled bower of blossoms, streamers, fronds, wands and boughs, all competing with each other for space that barely exists. Perhaps this is the alchemy that makes our garden the Elysium that many visitors find when they discover our valley.

Foxglove are growing everywhere. Some years I weed out the common pink ones from the cultivated areas and plant pale apricot and white ones. When they bloom the following year I am enraptured by their purple-spotted pallor but never get around to planting more. Consequently, the proliferation of the apricot and white foxgloves is constantly diluted by wildings. But these also captivate me for they are childhood flowers and, like the foxes, I love to wear the downy pouched flowers on my finger tips. The bees love them, too, and whine frantically as they dive headfirst into the warm dark bosom of the pollen-laden bells.

In our field the foxgloves are laced around with dainty white lesser stitchwort whose ten petals are no thicker than an embroidery thread. Bossy sorrel pushes up between them, and tall, stiff-stemmed plates of white yarrow flowers bob around the tall pink spires. But in the dappled woodland, foxgloves flower quite differently. They are taller, paler and more languid. Their companions are swarms of gnats, drooping azure-blue comfrey bells, giant mints, ferns, peaky campions and alkanet. Perhaps the recollection of early childhood foxgloves enchants me most. They grew along the edge of the woods and I would lie among them staring up at a blue sky and listening to the drunken whine of bees. If I happened to see a pink bell free itself from the loose clasp of the green calyx and tumble softly to the ground I was certain that some magical force was involved, for that was the world that constantly threatened, and yet at the same time seduced me. Ted Hughes' poem "Sunstruck Foxglove" is bewitching and I love the concept of his sultry gypsy foxglove.

> *As you bend to touch*
> *The gypsy girl*
> *who waits for you in the hedge*
> *Her loose dress falls open.*
>
> *Midsummer ditch-sickness.*

The azure sky is cloudless and hot sunshine has warmed the sodden soil and opened the flowers. After days of rain I am as thankful as the flowers to see the sun again. Even the birds seem happier and are chatting contentedly among themselves. The rugosa roses are blooming, and they thrive in a garden where roses are not generally happy. The perfumed dark carmine petals of 'Roseraie de l'Hay' dry beautifully and retain an oppulent perfume. They are perfect for use in potpourris. The white rugosa rose 'Blanc Double de Coubert' projects her sultry sweet perfume and causes all those who pass her to bury a nose in the soft chalk-white petals. 'Blairii No. 2', an old climbing rose, appears to have no objection to our garden either and the strong fragrance of her enormous double pink-petaled blooms stirs the imagination, recalling the roses of childhood.

The threepenny-bit rose is showing pink at the tip of her elegant pointed buds and now is the time to press these tiny blossoms which are the smallest of all the roses. The bush itself is quite large, though, and mine has reached at least 6 foot in height. I use the blossoms from this rose in my collages almost more than any other flower and the pink buds, surrounded by five elongated twisted sepals, add a delicate quality to any picture. For years I have decorated scented calico sachets with the fern-like foliage and long-stemmed buds. The buds are also exquisite arranged in formal rows and I have created many of my more ethereal collages within a border of these roses. Mixed with pressed forget-me-nots, enchanting garlands can be arranged on cards, sachets and gift tags. Sadly, the threepenny-bit rose is not easy to obtain and a good substitute is *Rosa multiflora*. Although the plant is a rampant climber, the buds of this rose are extremely small and they press well.

Cornwall is not an area known for its roses but I am still able to grow most of my favorites. The climbing "blue" rose 'Veilchenblau' scrambles over the front of the cottage, her mauve-striped flowers filling the bedrooms with a sweet violet perfume. 'Cécile Brunner', with her tea rose blossoms, rampantly climbs the side of the cottage and her peppery-sweet flowers never fail to captivate me with their diminutive perfection. Around the garden flop indispensable purple 'William Lobb', 'Tour de Malakoff', 'Céleste', 'Raubritter', 'Souvenir du Dr Jamain', the 'Apothecary's Rose', *Rosa gallica* and a host of unnamed centifolia, cabbage and damask beauties. Rampaging over the barn, up the sycamore and ash trees and into the neighbor's garden is banana-scented 'Kiftsgate' – a rose of immense growth whose racemes often hold aloft as many as 300 palest yellow roses.

Summer would not be complete without its lavender. Sadly I cannot grow it in my damp soil so I always gather mine from elsewhere. The rosebuds are those of the 'Threepenny-Bit' rose and I have mixed them with a few blossoms of lilac 'Sensation'.

ORIENTAL POSTER

*H*ere is a large collage inspired by the Orient. The beautiful water-colors of China and Japan, so often executed in shades of gray and black, fired me with enthusiasm. I envisioned a fresh new concept of design and color but, as with all new ideas, the vision was not easy to execute. However, through manipulation and rearrangement, a collage emerged that I believe evokes the atmosphere of Oriental art.

PREVIOUS PAGE
This large collage, in sombre shades, is reminiscent of a Chinese watercolour. The austere black irises and drooping Clematis durandii *blossoms have the restrained elegance of the flowers beloved by Oriental artists.*

Before laying out the botanicals, colorwash the background card in shades of gray and then cover it with black silk tulle. The tulle can be held in place by a covering of spray adhesive applied to the colorwashed card.

Then arrange the flowers, leaves and lichens, gluing them in place with rubber cement. Group pressed scabious, knautia, species clematis, *Cosmos atrosanguineus* and anaphalis together and then add spikes of buddleia, *Primula vialii*, polemonium, astilbes and *Clematis durandii*. These flowers all have unusual subdued coloring.

To complete the whole, add pads of gray lichen and scatterings of cow parsley florets. Two beautiful blossoms of the darkest purple *Iris sibirica* and some lavender spikes in the bottom right-hand corner are the finishing touch.

🌾 Ebony the cat now spends a lot of time in the garden. Her nose twitches at the exciting smells and her whiskers draw forward. Tiptoeing down the drive toward the barn she runs the gauntlet of the swallows who divebomb her to within an inch of her back. Unruffled, she continues her dainty walk past the barn and then sharp right along the banks of the river and into the wildest areas. There she must find the feline Elysian fields where the perfumes are those of mice, voles, shrews, rabbits and all the rank weeds. Often when she returns she brings with her the smell of ground elder, bindweed and damp earth.

🌾 To me, our two acres has an enchanted beauty of its own and the garden is now abundant with small arbors and bowers. Within them there is a world apart. Sitting down by the river, my chair is ensnared by purple loosestrife, 4-foot fondant-pink astilbes, scented Himalayan cowslips, monkey flower, yellow filliform-petaled *Inula hookeri* flowers and the white shepherd's-crook blossoms of *Lysimachia clethroides*. In this steamy damp area of the garden the gunnera leaves are 9 feet high and 6 or 7 feet across. They create a strange prehistoric atmosphere, and the filtered green light beneath them encourages lanky growth and bleaches the flowers. Desirable white *Polygonum campanulatum* (much prettier than the more common pale pink form) has spread beneath and around the gunnera. In an effort to escape the shade cast by the immense leaves, the polygonums' long jointed stems almost crawl toward the light where they emerge in a forest of ribbed leaves and white French-knotted blossoms. Here the gold-tinselled and lapis lazuli damsel-flies alight in their dozens. With two pairs of lacy wings folded immaculately above their iridescent bodies they sit motionless on the leaves, each one facing the sun.

The sun dapples the pale, lichen-coated trunks of the willows and around their base the mosses creep. In shafts of sunlight the peaty waters of the river expose their tenants and speckled brown trout, granite bedrock and fibrous willow roots can be seen. Damsel-flies are partial to the cool air above the water and their phosphorescent thin forms can be glimpsed darting upstream where the water's agitation is mirrored in the overhanging branches. The steps into the river are carpeted and hidden by streamers of rampant *Geranium procurrens*. Soon the dusky-violet, black-centered flowers will festoon the long banners of scented leaves that are already dipping their toes in the water. They will struggle to gain a foothold as the current pulls and tugs them downstream.

70

The perfumed air of the garden changes with each step and on the breath of the wind more sweet fragrance is diffused:

> *choice spices and every kind of aromatic thing, musk,*
> *amber, transparent tears of mastic, unrefined benzoin,*
> *and essence of every flower, camphor, coriander,*
> *cardamoms, cloves, cinnamon from Serendibis, Indian*
> *tamarind and ginger –*

THE ARABIAN NIGHTS

What fragrant dreams are woven around these aromatics of the pharmacy of *The Arabian Nights*. With the exception of musk and amber, I use them all in my potpourris and love the sense of history and romance that their poetic names impart. Sometimes I drop a fragrant "tear" of resin on the hotplate of the woodburning stove, and the whole cottage will fill with an incense, evoking the swinging incensors of the high church of my early years. Our warm humid summer garden is more fragrant than any other I know. Perfume hangs undispersed within the boundaries of the sheltering willows, bamboos, grasses and giant herbage. I am unable to grow many of the highly fragrant Mediterranean plants as our garden is too damp, but I am continually discovering other delicious aromatic flora that will tolerate our moist acid soil.

High in a chicory-blue sky a buzzard circles and floats on the thermals. The tiny black speck of a skylark quivers her wings and trills; perhaps she should, as the poets have suggested, build her nest on a cloud. Not far above the cottage and barns, broods of swallows swoop and slide through the sea-rinsed Cornish air. Their fun takes them nosediving to within a few inches of the roofs when they roll, turn and twist between the branches of the liriodendron and crab apple and arrive, precisely orientated, at the barn door. They are quite silent as they perform their aerobatics but once inside the barn give two chirrups and a warble. The garden is already full of the whisperings of mature high summer for many of the giant reeds and grasses are already 9 feet tall and their drooping strap like leaves brush one against the other. Even some of the tall meadowsweets murmur as their tough leaves quiver and rasp.

Riotous color has now left the flower borders. They have become verdant Rousseau paintings of greenery where summer's late flowers thinly decorate a profusion of growth. The immense fertility of the garden has now fully manifested itself, and in the filtered light I am immersed in a soft green flood. The woods, fields and hedgerows have lost their chintzy summer flowers too, and gentle greens diffuse over the valley.

For many years I have collected old bottles. Hundreds have been amassed and in order to find somewhere attractive to display them I have arranged them on an old railway sleeper outside the barn. Some old clay pots, emulsioned in bright colours, are filled with fuchsias, ivies and brightly flowered succulents.

FLOWERPOT COLLAGE

*I*nspired by the mossy flowerpots stacked in the potting shed, I decided to attempt a large collage of a mossy flowerpot. From this came the idea to make the column of flowerpots featured below.

For the large collage, draw the outline of a pot on a sheet of card and cut it out. Colorwash it a terracotta color and cover it with skeletonized leaves.

Around the base of the pot, glue some moss and then glue the pot onto a sheet of backing paper. I used fine mulberry handmade paper.

The contents of the pot can then be arranged. Pressed ivy and muehlenbeckia tendrils fall naturally out of it and the middle is filled with potentillas, cotton lavender flowers and tassels of cyperus flowers. Rubber cement is used throughout.

For the column of flowerpots, colorwash a sheet of card in terracotta and cover it with skeletonized magnolia leaves. The pots are then cut from this card and glued to a strip of handmade paper.

There are endless possibilities for ways in which to fill the pots. Mixed colors, monochrome arrangements and even whole pressed plants are but a few ideas.

To add a textured appearance, intersperse the flowers with bobbles of cotton lavender and small dried berries.

74

Inspired by a Paul Klee painting, beautiful acid yellows, shocking pink, orange, red and tawny flowers embellish mouthwatering sherbet lemon and orange backgrounds. The picture is created from four separate sheets of card, three of which have squares cut from their centers in order to create the rich three-dimensional quality of this picture.

This morning I awoke to see the garden shrouded in translucent mist. Through the window's curtain of nodding clematis blossom I watched creamy sunshine filter through a vaporous cloud of shifting water droplets. Beaded gossamer had sewn the lilac to the rose, tangled the tendrils of the vine and looped the honeysuckle in filaments of palest gray. But moments of such beauty are ephemeral and the sun rose quickly in the Eastern sky, warming the world and evaporating the mists. In an early morning garden the newly emerged red admiral butterflies are crowding the honeyed buddleia blossoms and the bees are frantic to gather nectar from the helmetted flowers of the white balsam. Dragon-flies are on the wing and the first pink-flowered Japanese anemone has opened. Fleabane's yellow daisies wait to be pressed and early berries to be gathered. The sun warms my shoulders and the garden fills with daytime fragrance, but I know the season's days are numbered. Soon more time will be spent within the four thick walls of the cottage and summer will have withdrawn her abundance. But the rhapsody of the flowers, and the bosky woods and lanes can be recalled more clearly than moments from any other season.

> But still for summer dost thou grieve?
> Then read our poets, they shall weave
> A garden of green fancies still,
> Where they wish may rove at will,
> They have kept for after treats
> The essences of summer sweets,
> And echoes of its songs that wind
> In endless music through the mind.

THOMAS HOOD

PART THREE

AUTUMN

'*Shaking his languid locks*
all dewy bright
With tangled gossamer that fell
by night,
Pearling his coronet of corn.'
THOMAS HOOD

 Autumn creeps so gently into my wild Cornish garden that I am barely aware of its harbingers. The first daddy longlegs drift past unnoticed, and I mistake harvestmen for spiders. The rich sunshine seeps through the early morning mists onto a gossamer-strewn garden, and toadstools and bracket fungus have appeared overnight. The light is golden and the air moist and warm, aerial cobwebs brush my cheeks and suddenly I realize how long my shadow is, bouncing and bobbing at my side. My garden is a fecund, overgrown paradise and:

Today I think,
Only with scents – scent dead leaves yield,
And bracken and wild carrot's seed,
And the square mustard field . . . . . .

And smoke's smell too,
Flowing from where a bonfire burns
The dead, the waste, the dangerous,
Which all to sweetness turns.

EDWARD THOMAS

I marvel at the truth in the last two lines of this evocative poem for monkshood, henbane, pokeberry, hemlock, datura, foxglove and black and deadly nightshade are all poisonous plants whose foliage may well be dumped on our bonfire and "Which all to sweetness turns". What potent and magical names they have and what visions of sorcery and skulduggery they evoke. Some of the autumn fungi have equally powerful names with evil connotations, for who would dare to sample the death cap, fly or bug agaric, stinkhorn or the scarlet, white-spotted *Amanita muscaria*, without fear of death? On the other hand, chantarelles and bluets sound quite innocuous as, indeed, they are. The historical significance of the plant world is truly fascinating. Hippocrates, Theophrastus, Dioscorides Gerard, Parkinson and Linnaeus, as well as herbalists, alchemists, apothecaries, perfumers, witches, sorcerers and magicians, have each manipulated the richness of their imagination and perception to research, analyse, document and name the occupants of our natural world. In my Cornish garden, I grow many of the plants that fascinated these great minds centuries ago, often referring to them by the name given to each one at that time. How enriched my life is by just knowing that hemlock was gathered after nightfall by witches and used in their nefarious practices. "Root of hemlock digg'd i' the dark"; as goes the incantation of the three witches in *Macbeth*.

The brilliant colours of the fall are not seen in Cornish gardens. Our peninsular has a mild, damp climate and many areas have no frosts at all, so the autumn colours are very subdued. Our own garden is about 500ft (150m) above sea level and we do have a few frosts, but they are not frequent or prolonged enough to colour the leaves.

I am always surprised at the number of new and interesting botanicals that I find to press and dry as each season progresses. This autumn I have started to gather some of the berries that the garden and hedgerows have to offer. Many press and dry really well and some, such as the commonplace rowan berries, dry to shrivelled orange baubles if placed on a saucer in a warm spot. The color of these berries intensifies as they dry and I long to acquire the pink-berried form. I can just visualize tiny, shocking-pink, wrinkled fruits adding a dramatic touch to a flower frieze, or perhaps a clutch of them in an informal collage.

For a number of years I have diligently pressed brilliantly colored autumn leaves only to find that I never seemed to have a use for them. However, one has only to look at stylized friezes in the decorative arts to see that the leaf form is constantly being manipulated, and I have now taken to using my autumn leaves in formal borders where they look quite beautiful. I am only concerned that perhaps I have not pressed enough of them! When drying and pressing botanicals one is forced to examine everything very closely and I am constantly amazed at the diversity and complexity of nature. Recently I have taken to wearing my father's old magnifying eyeglasses when looking at plants in detail and now I see even more clearly the different textures of petals and leaves; the structure of a stamen quivering with a pollen-laden anther; minute styles, stigmas and ovaries; the exquisite and significant veining on a petal that must attract the pollinating bee or perhaps just a greenfly frantically wiggling its translucent legs.

By day, the thinning overhead leaves of early autumn allow more sunlight into my shady borders and the garden is redolent of damp and collapsing herbage. I used to hate the season that heralded grim old winter but now I love every month for its familiar order of things and they tie me to the rhythm of nature. Once again I am able to see the old granite boundary walls studded with pennywort and ferns, and gnarled blackthorns display the thorned tracery of their black, angular branches. A few shriveled sloes still cling to them, but the first gales will rip them from their thorny stronghold and send them careering across the fields. Birds' nests, long since deserted, become apparent as do the first signs of spring. The occasional primrose can be seen in the garden and the succulent, narrow leaves of the grape hyacinth are already a couple of inches high. In sheltered spots, there are even daffodil noses pushing through the soil.

DRIED HYDRANGEAS

*T*HE damp Cornish air and rich acid soil encourages the prolific growth of all species, varieties and cultivars of hydrangeas. I grow both lace-cap and mop-head kinds of hydrangeas in as many varieties and colors as the wilder parts of the garden will sustain. Because of the acidity of our soil there is a preponderance of vivid blue flowers, the ultimate dream of all those who garden in an alkaline area. *Hydrangea paniculata* is a more unusual species with large creamy white panicles of flowers; the loose-domed flower heads provide attractive material for dried flower arrangements.

All hydrangeas dry extremely well. If the blossoms are picked when dry and papery then a day or two of hang drying will suffice.

It is best to arrange those flowers that are still soft in a vase of water and allow them to dry out slowly as the water evaporates.

If picked when dry and really crisp, hydrangeas should come straight from the garden into their containers.

Mounds of wonderful electric blue hydrangeas grace our late summer and early autumn garden. There are also pink, dark red, green and white blossoms. Here, the subtle muted colors and papery matt texture of the abundant blossoms are a delicate contrast to the patina of the old oak bread hutch.

INDIAN COLLAGE CARDS

Patience is essential for making cards such as these as it can be extremely painstaking work, particularly if ornamenting a card with columns of minute elderflowers or tiny marble-like seeds. But the end result is so gratifying.

*T*HERE is nothing more exciting, nor rewarding, than card making. During a day, perhaps a dozen diminutive collages can be made and I am always convinced that the one that I am working on is going to be infinitely better than the one just finished!

For some time I had wanted to make really flamboyant and decorative cards reflecting the gorgeous colors and intricate ornamentation of Indian crafts. I had also been intrigued by Indian floral patterns feeling that they could be the inspiration for unusual cards. Knowing that the muted colors of dried and pressed flowers would not be bright enough, I decided to create vibrant colors in the background and ornament them with dried botanicals.

Paint the cards with a wash of the bold colors of India using stripes, chequers and lattices in dazzling colors, or plain washes in vivid monochrome hues.

Add the ornamentation which can be fairly formal and repetitive, with the botanicals arranged in vertical, diagonal or horizontal bands.

As always, texture is important for it casts shadows and gives depth to an otherwise flat arrangement. Use small pressed and dried flowers, leaves, seeds and even whole spices to achieve this effect.

To achieve a stylized formality to the overall concept, incorporate single petals, half flowers and small sections of stalk into the design. The smallest botanical scraps can also be used, and if the color is not bright enough, then an occasional spray of metallic paint adds color to the odd row of flowers.

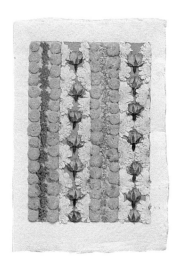 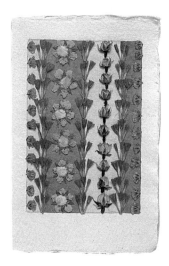

84

Many of the summer flowers also persist, surviving until the first frosts. Bouncing Bet frolics over everything, her pretty, disordered blooms masking the pernicious hold she has on my flower border. Little white cyclamen display their fragile, flowers, so perceptively described by D.H. Lawrence when he observed:

> *Cyclamens, young cyclamens,*
> *Arching,*
> *Waking, pricking their ears*
> *Like delicate very-young greyhound bitches*
> *Half yawning at the open, inexperienced*
> *Vista of day,*
> *Folding back their soundless, petalled ears*

I delight in those words for I always stop to gaze at their shy form.

Autumn has seen the arrival of Miss Suet Pudding, the dearest rescued tabby cat. Known affectionately as Suet she is plump, short-legged and banded in dark mackerel stripes. Prowling through my borders, she looks like a real tiggy tiger. To appease Ebony we have bought a trendy wickerwork cat basket, but unfortunately she loathes it as much as she loathes Suet. I have lined it with a tattered old pullover in the hope that its odiferous qualities will entice Ebony into the nether regions of her new basket. It remains to be seen whether or not my ploy works.

The little river remains a gentle stream, as it has been all through the summer. The quiet waterfalls are choked with yellow and orange willow leaves and the tough, hollow stems of water hemlock litter the banks. The depleted water is crystal clear as it slips over the dark mossy stones and trout have been trapped in the deeper pools. Extended families of long-tailed tits scour the overhanging trees for food. Their arrival is inevitably announced by an advance guard of three or four birds who hop from twig to twig uttering their thin "see see see" call. The swallows are gathering on the telegraph wires in large flocks and I know that any day their long, twittering song will no longer be part of my life as they depart on their long journey to Africa.

The wild hops are careering up our telegraph pole and now is the time I like to haul down the long, twisted swags of lettuce-green, scaly catkins. I dry them in our sitting room and they look beautiful draped over the top of the fireplace and along the shelves of the old oak dresser. I always want to leave them there for they evoke a pagan celebration.

During the autumn, the jewel-bright de Caen anemones arrive in the florists. I love their flamboyance, and arranged in a group of old blue glass bottles, their colors appear even more dramatic. I have decorated the inside of the box lids with miniature posies of dried flowers that reflect the botanicals used in the potpourri.

ANEMONE POTPOURRI
IN A DECORATED TIN BOX

I LIKE all monochrome flower mixes, and the contrast between the quaint fluffy scraps of cockscomb and luscious satin-petaled anemone blossoms is fascinating. Selecting and arranging the flowers of a pot-pourri can be just as enjoyable as the conception and execution of a grand botanical picture, for artistry enters into it all. Using flowers with no natural fragrance is interesting for one is then left free to experiment with unusual essential oils.

Anemones dry extremely well in silica gel crystals and their black-centered blooms transform any potpourri into an exquisite floral tapestry.

Perfume this mixture with sweet scents from the Orient, sharpened by the tangy fragrance of bergamot.

As this is a dry potpourri, mix all ingredients together, adding the essential oils last. It should then be put into an airtight container and stored for about six weeks, shaking daily.

1 quart mixed cockscomb and
anemone flowers
1 oz fine-ground gum benzoin,
orris root power or crushed
coriander seeds
2 oz lavender

1 tbsp mixed dried citrus peel
1 vanilla pod, chopped
2 drops ylang-ylang oil
2 drops lavender oil
2 drops bergamot oil

BASKET OF AUTUMN BOTANICALS

THE vibrant color, shape and texture of the fruit, vegetables, berries, leaves and spices give this display its character. I was inspired by the exciting colors of the unfaded, reverse side of an old kilim carpet. I used it to line a large basket and then had the fun of searching for some delicious botanicals to fill the container.

Autumn supplies sunset-colored pumpkins and pale, warty gourds. Almost filling a basket, their rough skins, exquisitely blotched and streaked in shades of umber, orange, yellow and apricot, and occasionally green, look beautiful against a kilim.

Parrotia leaves, turning to a shade of carmine, look lovely nestling among the pumpkins, as do ochrous rowan and vermilion cotoneaster berries.

Crackly dried Chinese-lanterns, tangerines, a few dried oranges, purple satin-skinned onions and a prickly-pear all carry through the vivid coloring of the kilim, at the same time their different textures add to the overall richness of the display.

To complete the arrangement, add bundles of cinnamon sticks, pomanders and pine-scented fir cones.

Purple and orange, acid-yellow and green, brown, shocking pink and black are combined in this old rug to give a brilliant tapestry of colour. I love this mixture of glorious and often clashing colours reflected in the basket of botanicals; they remind me of an Eastern market.

The small green flowers of the wild hop are more appealing than the larger cream ones that are used in the brewing of beer. The wildling has more grace and charm, and keeps its color when dried. The twisting stems, decorated with scaly cones, press well, and together with pressed and dried autumn fruits and berries, they can be used to border lavish seasonal collages.

The skies of dawn and dusk are now thinly veiled by autumn clouds, but in the evening the westering sun still bathes the Cornish landscape with its fiery glow. Occasionally I walk along the ridge of our little valley and gaze at the old miners' cottages, ancient farmhouses and granite barns that embroider the surrounding windswept fields and wetlands. Washed by the evening sun and orchestrated by the sheep and their lambs it becomes heart-breakingly beautiful.

Much of the remaining upright vegetation has now dessicated to thin, papery tissue. The dry, ribbon-like leaves of the tall grasses rustle and jostle in the gentle wind. The giant reed, *Arundo donax*, now stands 12 feet high and I love its enormity and elegance. The fluttering of its agitated leaves is like the swishing of a taffeta ball gown. I grow as many bamboos as I can, even though some are wickedly invasive, and they too whisper and murmur in the autumn garden. They all contribute to the Asiatic atmosphere that my garden evokes. In the overgrown pond, the striped rush, which is at least 6 feet high, has advanced another 4 feet into its neighbour's territory. The cream-banded leaves are turning pale apricot but soon their charm will be lost to the Cornish gales. The tasseled, almond-green flowers of the *Cyperus alternifolius* are just beginning to bronze and they must be picked and pressed. Recently I was peering at one of these tassels through my magnifying glasses and was fascinated by the extraordinarily meticulous and geometric arrangement of the florets. Their structure is identical to raised fishbone stitch in embroidery and momentarily I was quite subdued with the wonder of it all.

At long last Ebony has christened her new basket. As her dislike of it has been so evident more was my surprise when I found her peacefully ensconced in it, with a somewhat sheepish look on her face. She has obviously discovered that it is not so bad after all and, best of all, the basket really is far too small for the plump Suet to get inside.

AN IRONSTONE PITCHER OF FLOWERS

I KEPT the different elements of this arrangement grouped together, where their visual impact would be greatest.

❧ The berries are the hips of the *Rosa filipes* 'Kiftsgate' that climbs over our barn. An absolute giant of a climbing rose, its prolific racemes of pale yellow flowers smell of bananas. In addition to the attractive summer blossoms, 'Kiftsgate' keeps its hips throughout the winter, and they can be picked for indoor decoration over a period of about five months.

❧ At the back of the arrangement are two velvety heads of the extraordinary cockscombe, which is exactly what they resemble. Wheat and an unusual black-whiskered barley also feature here.

❧ Just the color alone of the brilliant orange Chinese-lanterns is captivating: pick them when there are still acid green and citrus yellow lanterns dangling on the stalks. They are exactly what is needed to lighten such an arrangement. I find that the simplicity and smooth surface of the pale, pewter-gray minarets of poppy seedheads contrast well with the other, more intricate, botanicals featured in this simple and yet very effective autumn arrangement gathered from my garden.

The patchwork quilt is made out of glazed chintz and is dated 1838. I bought it about 15 years ago, finished all but one border, complete in its owner's sewing basket, with unused scraps of material, threads and even the old templates made of eighteenth-century church accounts. I had great joy in completing the one border and it is now one of the "old characters" of our sitting room.

RED PANELED PICTURE

I ENJOYED making this collage and the end result still gives me pleasure. I had an inner vision that was fiery, theatrical and slightly wicked, rather like Bizet's Carmen! Certainly, the scarlet washed background covered with black silk net (wrinkled like a chorus girl's stockings) gives it a slightly scandalous air.

Paint four strips of white card with a wash of red watercolor or acrylic paint, diluting the color for each panel. Apply a spray glue to the panels, stretch and press silk tulle over them. Cream or white net is very simple to dye and a slightly streaky result can be rather interesting.

Assemble a selection of black, dark red, purple, mauve, orange and pink flowers, together with some textured mosses, lichens, seedheads and catkins in shades of green, orange and black. Starting with the darkest panel, and working from the bottom upward, arrange the botanicals, and when you are sure that you like the effect, lightly glue them in place.

On the first panel, use the darkest flowers, keeping the mosses and lichen at the base, where the botanicals were most thickly arranged.

On the second panel, keeping the mosses and lichens again at the base, arrange some brighter flowers.

The third and fourth panels are arranged in a similar manner, using progressively paler flowers more thinly distributed. As each panel is completed it is worth working on the next one with the previous one alongside. This will ensure that there is a continuity to the picture.

. . . .
PREVIOUS PAGE
The style of this collage
is slightly Oriental; I
find a lot of inspiration
in Japanese and
Chinese art and
embroidery.

The morning skies are still misty forget-me-not blue, but as I walk down our lane, thin wafers and ribbons of mist hang over frost-starched fields. It is 9:30 am and my shadow is 14 feet long. There are hawthorn hips and blackberries, alder catkins and cones, whiskered bobbles of sheep's-bit scabious, campions, yarrow, and sheaves of strangling white morning glory in the hedgerows. Although the common ivy is not recognized as a scented plant I am always made aware of its presence by a pervading sweet smell; perhaps it is the nectar produced so copiously by its flowers. Today, the winter gnats find the green knobbly umbels irresistible, or perhaps they just use them as a meeting ground for a wild dance! The dark, newly plowed fields are covered in a canopy of cobwebs that shimmer and glisten in the sunshine and even in the middle of a 12-acre field there is a profusion of gossamer. As autumn advances, our cottage becomes visible for it is no longer blanketed by the thick foliage of roses, clematis, akebia, vines, honeysuckle, pittosporum, *drimys*, myrtle, ivy, fatsia, and lilac.

The evenings are drawing in and I have more time to sit in front of the fire and dip into the many books that I use for research. Eugene Rimmel's *Book of Perfume* and G.W. Septimus Piesse's *The Art of Perfumery*, both printed in the last century, make for fascinating reading about the romantic history of scent and the science of perfumery. They even contain recipes that can be adapted for use today. The Egyptians were the first to document the art, using it in both their religious ceremonies and everyday life. They also used perfumes for embalming and mummification, for all fragrant botanicals have germicidal and preservative qualities. As the Egyptians believed in the transmigration of the soul it was imperative that their bodies were kept intact after death so that the spirit could return to its original body after visiting the bodies of many other living creatures. The soul might not be expected to return for several thousand years. The Bible refers to many rituals involving the use of fragrant oils and perfumes, the most historic in the documentation of Christianity being when Mary anointed Christ's head with oil of spikenard, wiping the surplus away with her hair. I find it all so fascinating and I particularly like to think that I am participating in the rituals of the ancient perfumer (but not, of course, the embalmer!) by growing and gathering the same plants. Many of the sweet herbs and juniper, orris root, sweet flag, roses, cedar wood, cassia, and frankincense and myrrh, are aromatics whose names we are familiar with which were used by the ancient civilizations.

LARGE POSY OF FLOWERS

A big posy of flowers gathered from an early autumn garden.

*T*HIS is the kind of arrangement where herbs, seedheads, garden flowers and even a few wild flowers can all hobnob one with the other. Even little faded-to-brown spindle berries have been used which add interesting contrast to thin-petaled flowers.

Make the silky cream background by gluing fragile seedpods to a sheet of white card.

The outline of the posy is quite symmetrical and the construction is carefully planned. Large flowers must balance groups of smaller blossoms and flower spikes should be evenly dispersed around the edge of the bouquet. Colors must be carefully mixed and distributed, and it is best to have a preponderance of only one strong color.

The outline of the picture is best made first, and it should be pretty and not too crowded, mixing round blossoms with sprays and flower spikes.

Only put a spot of rubber cement on the back of the center of the flowers and just a little on the lower half of the flower spikes. This will ensure that your arrangement looks free and natural, and slightly three dimensional. There is nothing worse than a flower collage that looks rigid.

Working towards the center of the picture, the posy can then be completed, always remembering that contrast of texture is as important as the mixing of subtle color and the overall design. The stalks can be added last. The final balance of the picture will depend upon the length of these stalks, so arrange a few and stand back and assess your picture before gluing them down. If you wish, add a little bow, but it is not absolutely necessary.

VETIVER GARLANDS
AND POTPOURRI-FILLED BOXES

*T*HE potpourri-filled boxes and rose-decorated garlands are made from the violet-scented roots of vetiver, or couscous. A native plant of tropical India, the roots used to be woven into sunshades. Sprayed with water in the heat of the day they released a cooling, sweet perfume. Vetiver is now made into all sorts of decorative objects, and I like the natural feel and look of the tough hairy roots, and their long-lasting fragrance.

The tiny vetiver garlands can be decorated with any pretty dried flowers and I used single pink roses. They can equally well remain unadorned, for their roots have a visual charm of their own. Attach the roses to the garland using rubber cement.

The potpourri is a spicy rose mix which blends well with the vetiver. All the ingredients of this dry potpourri can be mixed together at the same time and then allowed to mature, in an airtight container, shaken daily for six to eight weeks. The recipe is as follows:

1 quart dried whole roses
*   and buds*
2 oz lavender
1 oz orris root powder, crushed
*   gum benzoin or cumin seeds*
1 tsp cinnamon
2 tsp whole cloves
½ tsp ground allspice
½ tsp nutmeg
4 drops rose oil
2 drops lavender oil
1 drop patchouli oil

98

Autumn is the time for clearing, weeding and dividing; with one's nose so close to the earth it is also a time to examine and sniff roots. There are many plants with fragrant roots and each year I discover more. Sweet flag, Florentine iris, angelica, elecampane, herb bennet, *Geranium macrorrhizum*, sweet Cicely, roseroot and astrantia have deliciously fragrant roots which can be lifted, dried and used in potpourris. It would be interesting to make a potpourri of nothing but scented roots, adding a few spices, one or two citrus pomanders and perhaps a few drops of pine and frankincense oil. Now is also the time to pick a few last leaves from the scented leaf pelargoniums. No other leaf in the plant kingdom can smell quite so mouthwateringly sweet. I would suggest that if you have a greenhouse or conservatory, and like scented botanicals, then grow as many varieties as you can. *Pelargonium capitatum* and *P. graveolens* smell of roses, *P. crispum* of lemon, *P. clorinda* of eucalyptus and *P. tomentosum* (so charmingly described by Gertrude Jekyll as having "leaves as thick as a fairy's blanket") of peppermint. These are just a few of the highly scented varieties.

This dainty ornamental grass displays its thin, cordlike leaves in a fountain of pale yellow and russet. Inconspicuous but appealing flower heads appear in early autumn and their cream tassels have the tousled look of a recent blow-dry! I like all ornamental grasses and this one, by virtue of its graceful and drooping structure, deserves to be placed somewhere uncrowded. Although I do not grow it in the granite chippings of the yard area, I know that in such isolation it would be seen at its best.

Many of the crab apples are now ripening and some of the dark red varieties have beautiful pink flesh. Cut in wafer-thin slices, they press extremely well and just one translucent, pink slice can decorate a card. Many tropical fruit and vegetables are now available, and it is always worth experimenting with them. Cut into thin slices and pressed with care (changing the paper at least once a day), many will retain their color and shape. They look most unusual ornamenting cards and posters, but ensure that they are annotated for not everyone is able to identify a small cross section of okra or a pressed snowpea!

The arrival of the spiders has commenced. Each autumn sees droves of spiders invade our cottage, swelling the numbers of those already ensconced along the beams, over the ceilings and in every nook and cranny. Skirmishes break out in the hallway where space is at a premium. Baby spiders vie with tiny spiders, who vie with short- and medium-legged spiders, who vie with long-legged spiders for a spot on the ceiling, preferably in the corner. The moment arrives when I know that something must be done about the arachnid population, but like many other people, I wouldn't dream of killing a spider. So I try to vacuum them up and then empty the contents of the cleaner in the garden, just to give them a sporting chance. Unfortunately, many have a tenacious hold when confronted with a strong indraft of air. I usually manage to get about a third of them outside and they are back the following morning. I don't really mind for I am quite fond of them, but housewifely duty can said to have been done.

Margery Fish's scintillating Michaelmas daisy has survived the first frosts but her spindly, coal-black stems can no longer support the cornucopia of blossoms. She has collapsed in a heap of blooms and arms and legs. In the struggle to hold her flowers aloft she has created a low bobbing bed of ultraviolet blossoms, all pushing up between dead and decaying growth. The whole effect is quite delightful and next year I shall push her over, just in case she doesn't fall.

The prevailing southwesterly winds are tugging and pulling at the top of the trees, warning of the gales to come. The last remaining leaves have been wrenched from the branches and, as the winds strengthen, are sent hurtling down our lane. The starlings have started to flock and blacken the evening sky as tens of thousands fly overhead making for their roosting trees on the other side of the valley.

TUMBLING BOUQUET

*T*HE twisted stems of lettuce-green wild hops, dense white heads of anaphalis buds and trailing wands of fluffy gray *Clematis tanguitica* seedheads make a beautiful tumbling bouquet. The pale greens, grays and white give this unpretentious bouquet a cool charm. This is no contrived or titivated arrangement of the flowers and seedheads, and they were tied together with raffia just as I gathered them from the garden. Leaning on the granite wall beside the bouquet is a lichen-encrusted stick reflecting all the greens, grays and white shades of the bouquet. Examining and identifying each lichen on the stick is a botany lesson in itself.

The most interesting lichen is the tufts of oakmoss (*Evernia prunastri*), which smells of dusty violets and plays such an important role in perfumery. The essential oil that it contains helps to stabilize the scent of other perfumes, thereby prolonging the life of any mixed bouquet of perfumes.

The tumbling bouquet was photographed in the woods near our house which run down to a boulder-strewn river whose water once turned the wheels of a long line of mills used in the manufacture of gunpowder. The old granite mills are now almost hidden by great swags and falls of ivy, colonies of ferns, lush cushions of moss and over-hanging trees, and it is one of the most hauntingly beautiful places that I know.

Immigrant redwings have arrived and nervously feast on the hawthorn berries. The blackbirds cry "pink" at dusk; perhaps they object to the peace of bedtime being disturbed by a prowling human, but I love to hear their "pink pink pink". It takes me back to my childhood and a little thatched cottage nestling in a lichen-covered orchard that seemed to be full of blackbirds.

Our bedroom window is always kept open at night for to feel at peace I must hear the rushing of the river in my ears and have cool air on my face. I like listening to the animal noises, too, especially the tawny owl when he perches in the overhanging branches of the sycamore tree and utters his shrill "kuvvitt kuvvitt". More than anything else I love to lie in bed with the Cornish gales roaring and shrieking outside above the slate-tiled roof of the cottage:

> *wild sorceress, me thy restless mood delights*
>
> JOHN CLARE

The bedroom door struggles to free itself and the windows frantically rattle on their latches. More frequently the winds are gentle and I am lulled by the familiar murmuring in the surrounding trees. John Clare must have found comfort in the winds at night:

> *Listening to the ushering charms,*
> *That shapes the Elm trees mossy arms*
> *Till soft slumbers stronger creep*
> *Then rocked by winds I fall asleep.*

Time moves on and now all the late autumn flowers are over. *Aconitum carmichaellii*, cimicifugas, black chocolate-smelling *Cosmos atrosanguineus*, crocosmias, pretty mauve *Dahlia merckii*, highly poisonous pokeberry, lime green *Nicotiana langsdorfii*, nerines and massive *Eryngium lassauxii* are some of the unusual flowers that bloom in my autumn garden. The towering 5 foot flower spikes of *Aconitum carmichaelii* dry to a dull sky-blue and look beautiful when arranged with rusty brown dock seeds. A prolific wild flower which is late flowering and grows in the marshy areas of the garden is fleabane. Its yellow daisy flowers press beautifully, the fine petals becoming threadlike, and I use it time and time again in my work. Because of the formality of its shape, it will often pull a ragged design together. Fleabane lives up to its name for the leaves can also be dried and used as an insect repellant. Growing with it is gray-leaved sneezewort, another late flowering marsh lover. The old names for these plants are self-explanatory and their humble beauty and history is quite captivating. I have grown more and more

The flower heads of Eryngium lassauxii from South America grows to a towering 10 feet in the rich moist soil of my garden. The rapier-like leaves and huge heads of pale-green, thimble-like flowers have unusual grace and form for such a giant plant, and it has become a much admired occupant of the autumn garden.

of these wildlings and when I look at them I see not only their simple charm, but think of their role in the ancient world of herbal lore and medicine.

There are no longer any of the autumn butterflies around. Red admirals, small tortoiseshells, commas, common blues, small coppers and large whites all visited the late-flowering plants in the garden, field and wood. How fortunate we are to have them.

Gales and torrential rains have now transformed the landscape and our river. The smell of decaying vegetation is everywhere, the garden is sodden and the waterfalls are glassy slides of peaty floodwater. All the dead foliage has been washed away from the banks of the stream and the meandering path of the river can be seen quite clearly. There are still hips, haws and berries around and the leafless hawthorns and willows have exposed moss- and lichen-covered trunks supporting prolific colonies of pennywort, ferns, wood sage and foxgloves. Our Cornish air is always damp and this encourages the spreading plant kingdom around the base of the trees to slowly make its way up the trunk, rooting as it goes in the soggy lichen and moss.

Stray seeds that land on the upper branches germinate quickly in the humid conditions; I once had a colony of *Mimulus* growing in a willow tree! The damp also encourages the growth of algae and many of the hawthorn branches and all the oak apples are powdered with an almond-green meal. The jungle of giant gunnera that grows alongside the river in the lower woodland has succumbed to the frost and the great leaves have become tattered and black; hanging in veined folds they look like the sensitive ears of an old bull elephant. But their demise reveals the promise of spring for the crowns of this enormous plant already display great fat, pink-fringed buds that are at least 2 feet long.

Autumn has passed so quickly and I have loved all her moods. It is difficult to imagine the fragrance of a herb garden warmed by the sun, a wild damp jungle of herbaceous plants, butterflies, swallows and canopied shade; but that was the nature of autumn when I started writing this chapter. Now the bare bones of the garden and surrounding countryside are revealed. I can examine summer's nests, explore animal tracks and watch storms racing in from the Atlantic. I can dream of filling the meadow with cranesbills, columbines, white ragged robin and lady's bedstraw, and our woodland with bluebells, primroses, violets, orchids and lily-of-the-valley. Along the lane, fern and bracken fronds blanket the dormant spring flowers and water seeps from the fields flooding across the road. Rooks and seagulls scatter raucously across the blackening skies and a sparrowhawk flies fast and low over the hedgerows, searching for a hapless victim. Tomorrow is the first day of winter, and autumn shall be laid to rest.

This is an easy picture to create and could just as easily have been made with pretty spring flowers, pussy willows, hazel catkins and snail shells, or perhaps seaweeds and flowers and seedheads from the cliffs.

> *Forming with leaves thy grave,*
> *To sleep inglorious there mid tangled woods,*
> *Till parched lipped summer pines in drought away*
> *Then from thine ivied trance*
> *Awake to glories new.*

JOHN CLARE

PART FOUR

WINTER

'*The frost lies soft – and thick –*

and white

Upon the fields and in the air . . .

On poplar trees – as if in prayer

And Orchard – mystical –

apart –

The unborn Spring within her

heart . . '

ME MASON

108

Although there is a softness to the winter fields that surround the farmsteads of our valley, I am always conscious of a far wilder ancient moorland that skirts and borders the cultivated fields. Here the curlew delivers his haunting "curlee". It echoes across the valley, capturing in just two notes all the wild beauty of Cornwall. During the winter months, when the gnarled hawthorns of the moorland are bereft of their leaves, when dead bracken has exposed massive granite boulders, and bare stone walls cobble field and moorland together, the vestige spirit of primeval man can penetrate my very being. Within his stone circles and around his standing stones there hangs in the air a perception of his pagan gods, and in stormy darkness.

Night which Pagan Theology could make the daughter of Chaos, affords no advantage to the description of order.

GARDEN OF CYRUS

This is the pageantry of living within a land where legend still persists and of being receptive to its powerful charm.

When our boundary hedge becomes a transparent winter filigree, the blackthorn thicket no longer hides the lower marshy fields, and skies and winter corn can be glimpsed through the bare branches of the sycamores. The boundaries seem to be no more and a summer two acres becomes a winter two hundred acres. So it will remain until the exuberance of lush vegetation once again restrains my vision to within my legal confines. But it is over the two hundred acres that I love to watch the capricious Cornish winter unfold his vagaries; no longer is our garden a sheltered warm paradise for we are left exposed to the ever-changing elements of a peninsular climate.

Black-skied Atlantic storms can rush over the western horizon and sweep the valley, hurling clouds, hail, birds, leaves and branches across the width of the narrow peninsula, only to be followed moments later by an uneasy calm, a shy white sun and enough blue sky to make a sailor a pair of trousers (as the Cornish would say)! Very occasionally, wicked blizzards from the east hit Cornwall and force-ten gales can pile the snow high in our steep-banked lanes, isolate our valley and devastate the tender and sub-tropical plants in the garden. But I never mind too much for it is all the gardener's tale and puny would be the plantsman who could be put off by such adventures. However, these circumstances are more unusual and we generally enjoy mild, wet and stormy winters, with only a few frosts.

Frost still coats the grass and low mounds of leaves in a wintry and very bare garden. The soil is sodden and water lies along all the border edges. The majestic seedheads of phormiums are still upright, but behind them the stems of the giant reeds and grasses of the pond have buckled and giant gunnera leaves no longer hide the barn. Other than the bright green shoots of the old-fashioned day-lily, that emerge before the winter has barely begun, everything is underground.

BLACK AND WHITE ARRANGEMENT

*T*HERE are limitless possibilities with cards. I enjoy working within the discipline of black and white although here I have allowed a little pink to creep into my work.

The striped card was inspired by black and white ticking. Draw a pencil rectangle on the front of the card, add guidelines for the stripes and then fill them in with a diluted black watercolor paint. A draftsman's pen is ideal for fine lines. To complete the card, decorate the central black panel with cream and pink potentillas and roses, and small umbels of cow-parsley.

Make the collages separately and glue them to the front of the cards after they have been completed. Make the background by washing a sheet of white card with water. When the card has absorbed the water, drop and splash diluted and very diluted black watercolor paint onto it. Once the card is dry, cut it into rectangles the size required for the front of the folded card.

One card is decorated with black *Cosmos atrosanguineus* flowers, *Clematis viticella* buds and rose leaves, arranged quite haphazardly. The gold surround is painted on after the collage is glued to the card.

The other rectangle is decorated with a spray of *Clematis recta* previously sprayed with matt black paint attached to a background card. After gluing the small collage onto the card, surround it with a fine black line.

The potpourri is a mixture of black mallow flowers and pink rosebuds. It is a dry potpourri and the recipe is as follows:

1½ pints black mallow flowers   *1 tsp whole cloves*
½ pint whole pink rosebuds   *½ tsp grated nutmeg*
1 oz lavender   *4 drops rose oil*
1 oz orris root   *2 drops lavender oil*
few pieces dried lemon peel   *2 drops lemon oil*

Mix all the dry ingredients together thoroughly, add the essential oils and store for six weeks in an airtight container, shaking daily, before using. The perfume is traditionally rosy with a sharp hint of lemon.

Nestling among this collection are a scented cushion and sachet embellished with textured french and bullion knot embroideries of roses, forget-me-nots and leaves. Make casings of embroidered ticking and fill them with equal parts dried lavender, mint and rose petals.

SNOWDROP CANDELABRA

I HAVE had such joy from my pretty Third World candelabra. Five candles emit just enough soft light to illuminate the dining room. Decorated and perfumed white domestic candles are infinitely preferable to elaborately shaped candles in their simplicity.

These candles are decorated with pressed snowdrops. Hold the flowers in place with your thumb and lightly brush them with melted wax, to affix them to the candle. When the wax has hardened, dip the entire candle in melted scented wax.

If you wish to adorn candles in this way, the correct container for melting wax should be used and all safety precautions taken when decorating and burning the candles. Once lit, they should never be left unattended.

For days on end, low clouds can shroud the fields and moorland and incessant fine drizzle will saturate the lichen-strewn trees, winter herbage and moss-covered ground. Even fields of newly germinated winter corn can be dappled with puddles and interesting stones and shards will lie exposed on the surface of the soil. Suddenly the clouds will lift, exposing an azure sky, and the valley will drip and sparkle, basking in the slanting rays of an incredibly warm sun. Occasionally, the evening or night temperature will drop dramatically, and under a star-seeded sky frost will transform our garden and the valley into a white-crystalled world. I have known the frost to remain with us all day, stiffening the primrose and snowdrop stalks and destroying the foliage of more tender plants.

Winter evenings have a magic of their own and tucked up within the warmth and safety of the cottage we frequently find that there comes a moment,

> *When the words rustle no more,*
> *And the last work's done,*
> *When the bolt lies deep in the door*
> *And Fire, our Sun,*
> *Falls on the dark-laned meadows of the floor.*
>
> JAMES ELROY FLECKER

and of course the pussies are safe on our laps, their bubbling purrs gently resounding through our knees.

SUNFLOWER HEADS, DOCKS AND PATCHWORK

*S*UNFLOWER heads have a Mediterranean charm, and I never catch a glimpse of one without feeling the scorching sun of holidays in southern France. Picked just before the seeds ripen, they dessicate into gently contorted, upturned saucers. The tightly packed seeds are encased in a circle of diamond-shaped containers that are arranged in the most perfect symmetry, the whole being surrounded by an elegant pinked edge of dried petals.

Dried sunflower heads showing the intriguing symmetry of their structure and the subtlety of their cream, brown and black colouring.

Hanging in the background is a rough old patchwork, whose corduroys, worsteds, calicoes and twill reflect the colors of the dried botanicals. The discarded coarse shirts, tough work corduroys and "Sunday Best" suits worn by the old men from the local workhouse of my childhood have been put to good use in this simple old quilt.

Pile the brown and cream sunflower heads into an old roughly hewn wooden trough, both of which have a compulsive tactile quality.

Scour your local hedgerows in early winter for the sturdy, deep-brown seedheads featured here. The tall stems, heavy with their matte-brown seeds, look beautiful when mixed with a few spikes of the deep-blue *Aconitum Carmichaelii*. The docks and the aconitum are arranged in an old bleached oil can which has the same discarded feel as the feeding trough.

SEAWEED PICTURE

To give this picture more variation and color, I have added some green and yellow lichens, moss and some artificially colored jade-green anaphalis flowers.

THIS is the first large collage that I have made using seaweeds, beachglass (fragments of broken glass tumbled to smoothness by the sea), shells and pebbles.

To create the impression of a watery background, dye scraps of silk net sea-green, dark green and royal blue. Then stick the net onto a circle of stiff white paper covered with a layer of rubber cement, allowing the net to crumple and fold quite naturally. Use only one layer of net in places, and in others superimpose blue on green. The whole affect is very watery with the double areas of net giving the impression of currents and eddies.

Arranging the botanicals, shells, pebbles and glass to form a pretty, balanced picture takes time, and it is worth experimenting and rearranging a collage such as this a number of times. The densest area should be at the base, using lichens and moss with fronds of seaweed, shells, pebbles and sea glass. Toward the apex keep ornamentation sparser, using only a large and fragile frond of seaweed and some small pieces of beachglass. Finally, place the green anaphalis flowers around the edge of the lichen. Everything is glued in place with a rubber cement. Then trim around the edges and mount the collage on a sheet of rough-textured paper.

As everything collected from the beach is covered in salt, the seaglass, shells and pebbles need to be thoroughly washed. Seaweed has to be treated with care as many of the fronds are quite fragile. To keep them moist, collect specimens in a plastic bag, and rinse them thoroughly in cold tap water until all traces of salt water have been removed. Carefully dab them dry and then arrange them on the paper in which they are to be pressed, pulling them out gently to their pretty fronded structure.

Seaweed takes a long time to dry when being pressed. To speed up the process, I recommend that the empty sheets of paper between the sheet holding the seaweed be replaced daily by dry paper. The damp paper can be dried in a warm spot and reused many times over. In this way, the seaweed will dry in just a couple of weeks.

The winter garden, bare of most of its leaves and flowers, can be explored in depth and once again I can admire the charming form of our teardrop bed. Looking through the trees of the woodland, I wonder at their growth during the fifteen years since we planted them. Already the filigree leaves of the cow parsley have formed dainty mounds beneath their boughs. Our hedge of hawthorn, blackthorn, hazel, rowan, honeysuckle, sweet briar and wild cherry is thick and high and it is hard to recall the weekend when we planted that too, but in the scant winter landscape I can admire the satin-thin bark of the sturdy cherry trees, the tiny catkins dangling from the hazel bushes and the gaunt structure of the rowan trees. Now that the giant leaves of the gunnera have collapsed, the pond is visible and I recall with sheer delight the day that we all sat and watched the hose fill a large muddy crater that my husband had industriously excavated by hand. Our excitement was completed by the early arrival of a frog, whose instinct must have told him that in a dry summer half an inch of water is better than no water at all. Our pond is now a plantsman's and naturalist's paradise, full and overflowing with interesting and unusual flora and fauna. We almost take for granted the dragon and damsel flies; frogs, toads and newts; water shrews (and how pretty they are with their silver tummies) and voles; herons and wagtails, and the water beetles and pond skaters which now inhabit the pond. There is also a large and varied collection of hardy and half-hardy water and marsh plants.

The winter-flowering 'Soleil d'Or' narcissus is already in bloom on the Isles of Scilly and today my husband returned home clasping a large bunch of the small egg-yolk yellow, scented trumpets. Their powerful perfume fills the kitchen and already they have played their tricks on my olfactory nerves. The bouquet of their fragrance contains, among other chemicals, indole, whose fetid smell is present in the odor of decaying fish. The warmth of the kitchen increases the release of this chemical and for a moment I am tricked into believing that something rather horrible may be lurking within my home. Suddenly my nose captures the other more pleasing perfumes of the little narcissus and I take a deep breath and bask in its heady overall fragrance. How amazing the structure of the natural world is, and the closer I examine it the more am I overwhelmed by its complexity and order. Perfumery and its history totally enthrall me, and I dearly wish that more attention had been paid in the chemistry classes of my schooldays.

When we arrived here 15 years ago our garden was bare of trees. The first to be planted were the common alder which have thrived in the moist soil. In those early days they provided the only shelter from the prevailing south-westerly winds and without them the garden could never have been created. They are quite brittle, lanky trees and their late winter catkins are magnificent. Brought into the house early in the winter their catkins will expand further into knobbly, quaking catkins.

Beautiful frilled and puckered lichen growing on the trunk of a crab apple tree.

The perfume of the narcissus can be extracted in oil. The process is very simple and is that used by the ancient Egyptians. Immerse the narcissus in a stoppered bottle of almond or olive oil (my preference) or sesame or any vegetable oil. Leave the flowers in the oil for two or three days and then carefully remove and replace by further fresh blooms. Continue this procedure until the oil is strongly perfumed with the fragrance of the narcissus. Of course, you shouldn't be limited to narcissus blooms; any fragrant flowers, leaves, seeds, roots, woods or resins can be immersed in oil and their perfume extracted, although some botanicals will work better than others.

'Soleil d'Or' narcissi also press extremely well, retaining their bright yellow color. They do not fade with time either and can look charming in a collage of pussy willows, alder catkins, mosses, lichens and ivy. Just a single pressed spray used to decorate a card is beautiful, even more so if the card is colored with a wash of the palest of apricot.

BORDERS

There are many unusual uses for borders: they can be cut into sections, threaded with ribbon and used as gift tags; a vertical section can be used to decorate a card; small sections can decorate writing paper; a jumble of different borders, arranged in vertical stripes, will make a beautiful and unusual collage, and, of course, they are delightful surrounding any botanical picture.

THESE borders are reminiscent of any decorative ribbons, tapes, gimps, wallpaper borders, friezes or edgings. They are quite compelling to make for so many unusual effects can be created very simply. Inspiration can be gleaned from any of the decorative arts and very few botanicals are required in their making. Much of the fun is derived from the initial preparation of the strips of card. They can vary from very narrow to fairly wide and can be painted in a variety of stripes, geometric shapes, bordered in gold or silver or just washed over in a single color. With the exception of a fairly wild and random frieze of mixed flowers, borders should have a repetitive and formal design. Without that they lose their point and become jumbled, for their purpose is, after all, to complete an artistic concept.

Use many small fragments in work such as this. Individual flower petals and leaves divided into sections or even cut in half are most effective. Whole allspice, cloves, cardamom and star anise are excellent for repetitive work, adding substance to a design that lacks a positive element.

When arranging flowers and leaves there is no need to adhere to a pre-planned design. It is sometimes best to experiment with shape, texture and color until a pleasing design evolves. Knowing where the border is to be used will dictate the colors, but it is surprising how many of these quite different edgings could enhance the same picture.

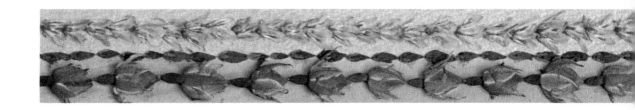

BASKET OF SILVERED FRUIT AND SEEDHEADS

I AM always motivated by the manipulation of color and texture whether in a collage, embroidery, flower arrangement or container of botanicals. I experience immense visual pleasure when I work and am quite prepared to take radical steps in order to achieve a desired effect.

For this arrangement I initially had only a vague idea of a silvered basket of botanicals. I visualized the thinnest veil of burnished silver, leaving exposed a glimpse of the original color of the botanicals.

Choosing the botanicals for such an arrangement is always a challenge and exciting. Stiff, mahogany-colored magnolia leaves, *Iris sibirica*, sea holly, and giant thistle seedheads and pine cones can be hunted down in winter gardens. Add to this a bowl of two-year-old dried oranges, lychees and other hard-skinned tropical fruit, some autumn gourds and a selection of nuts and it is time to experiment with the gilding.

Wax gilt polish is the only medium that creates an effect such as this; silver spray or paint leaves a harsh, unsubtle and overwhelmingly silver effect. So, using a fine, soft, watercolor brush twisted around in a jar of silver gilt wax, lightly brush the botanicals. Then finally polish them with a clean shoe brush, so adding to their luster.

Only add silver to the base of the pine cones and giant thistleheads as, viewed from that angle, their construction is so symmetrical and pretty.

Before arranging the basket, put a layer of dry pine sawdust, chunks of liriodendron wood and chopped angelica, elecampane and sweet Cicely roots in the bottom, sprinkling a few drops of myrrh and cedarwood essential oils onto them.

After arranging the seedheads, fruits, nuts and pine cones, fill in the gaps with some dried, old-fashioned roses because they lift the whole arrangement and look so beautiful. It is even worth adding a few pads of apple-green moss.

. . . .

PREVIOUS PAGE
The basket is displayed on a beautiful length of old silver lamé and pink chiffon fabric. The silver shoes are quite adorable, and to me even more precious than the antique fabric.

The first wax-tipped leaves of the snowdrops are pushing through the cold, moss-covered earth and mind-your-own-business is filling all the cracks and crevices around the cottage. Like drifting green snow it is making all unevenness even and carpets of it are obscuring the steps leading to the terrace. Some evergreen tellima leaves have turned bright carmine and the palest cream-veined ivy has climbed to the top of the terrace retaining wall, where its thin, translucent leaves hover like white moths. Scaled American currant buds are still slim and hug their stems, but large, papery packets of *Helleborus viridis* flowers are ready to eject their exquisite green flowers. Spectral remnants of quivering honesty pennies cling to their bleached stems but around them latent spring has already pushed the earliest daffodil leaves into the winter garden.

All the lowest areas of the garden are under an inch or two of water and so they will remain until the spring. I am always surprised at the health and vigor of the plants in these areas and even columbines, dicentra, sweet woodruff, Welsh poppies and bluebells will emerge happily from a winter in squelching mud. In the swampy areas of the valley, the emerald pads of moss have spread over all the bare earth around the roots of trees and up their trunks, over stones, and are even coating some of the thicker dead winter stalks. Interestingly, much will die back during the summer months, only to be replaced yet again next winter. The tightly packed leaves of the water hemlock have already emerged and the mounds of cow parsley leaves are about 6 inches high. The dried threads of the profuse, late summer-flowering bindweed still festoon the lower branches of the willows and pale, rust-colored bracken blankets the riverside areas of bluebells. Daisies, dandelions, primroses, heathers, campions, alpine strawberries, comfrey, pulmonaria, heartsease, mahonia and periwinkles are in bloom.

A full moon sails high in the cold dusk sky. The cobbles of the unused farm lane have been covered by weeds and my feet pad softly on the velvet ground. The farm is deserted and still but for the occasional rattle of a loose door and the quiet surprised chirrup of roosting birds. I feel privileged and alone. The old mounting block charges the imagination with visions of sturdy horses and heavy-booted riders. The low, humble farmhouse has seen generations of Cornish farmers come and go, and the crumbling, patched, granite barns have watched untold numbers of sheep, cows, pigs and horses live out their allotted time.

LICHEN-COVERED BRANCHES

I SEE no reason why bold botanical arrangements should not decorate the more sheltered parts of the garden, particularly the terrace. The lichen-festooned branches filling this old giant flower pot were gathered from a moorland tree uprooted by recent storms.

As well as the incredible fronds of long, hairlike lichen there are beautiful puckerings and tufts of daintier lichen clinging to the smaller twigs.

Incorporate as many shades of green as possible. Here they are quite exquisite, ranging from muted jade to pale almond, apple and even white with only the faintest hint of green.

The stone maiden is dressed in intricately decorated medieval clothes – I look forward to the day when algae stain her the color of the lichens.

. . . .
This photograph was taken after heavy rain and the lichens are swollen and heavy with moisture. Permeating the air around the arrangement there hangs the faintest smell of a sweet antiseptic which emanates from the sodden, hairlike lichen. There is an interesting array of crushed fossils in the lump of stone.

NEST OF FLOWER-DECORATED BROWN BOXES

*T*HIS nest of brown cardboard boxes was intriguingly attractive even before the boxes were decorated. They are covered in hand-made sepia and stippled paper, a pretty background to a haphazard arrangement of dainty flowers. After experimenting, I decided that racemes of creamy, pressed elder flowers, arranged sparsely and glued (using rubber cement) over the sepia background, looked slightly oriental and pretty, in a very discreet way.

So that the lids appear to be embroidered, it is necessary to create a more textured appearance. The pressed flowering heads of the water cyperus, superimposed over the elder flowers, resemble exquisite stem-stitched embroideries and add depth.

Finally, and still in a slightly oriental tradition, carefully glue a few creamy feverfew flowers and lavender heads in place.

The doors and windows are painted an unlikely shade of turquoise green, but the moonlight has drained all color from the buildings and their surroundings. Even in the gloaming I can see small ferns and newly sprouting tufts of nettles that have established themselves in every nook and cranny of the walls. Along the pigsty boundary lies heaped the old iron cleared from the farmhouse and its buildings. Corrugated iron, barbed wire and old paint cans lie rusting, as do more intimate beds, an old stove, jugs, pans and buckets. Five decrepit hay forks, six scythes, two hay-cutting knives, a selection of gate latches and some hand-wrought iron fencing reflect the social history of pre-war days and perhaps should be retrieved. I have a great affection for this old heap as, I believe, Edward Thomas had for his when he wrote,

> *The nettles cover up, as they have done*
> *These many springs, the rusty harrow, the plough*
> *Long worn out, and the roller made of stone.*

The settlement stands on the ridge of the valley and looks towards the southernmost tip of Cornwall and beyond to the wild Atlantic ocean. The air is colder and the winds stronger here; and life itself a little harsher than within the fold of the valley. Pad-padding like a donkey with his hooves wrapped in seaweed, I make my way down the track and away from the drovers' green roads of the hilltop farm. The sweet almond fragrance of winter heliotrope drifts along the lane and I pick a few of the tasseled flowers. Turning the corner the honeyed lights of the cottage diffuse through each small window, and I walk into the welcoming warmth of my kitchen. Winter heliotrope can become a pernicious weed, particularly in the warmer counties, but it has a sweet perfume and a fascinating half-mourning, white-lilac color. I have dried the blooms and used them in winter potpourris, but I prefer to have a mug of the fresh blossoms on my kitchen table.

Maidenhair spleenwort growing in the nooks and crannies of an old barn wall.

On Stygian nights the gales often roar across Cornwall. High in the nearby Monterey pines the gusts will reach storm force, and around the cottage they will be wild but not so fearful. The wind will boom down the chimney, whistle through the chinks of the woodburner and rattle the flue of the solid-fuel cooker. There will be a pervading smell of hot metal as our fire roars. Suddenly the storm will pause for breath, only to continue seconds later with renewed vigour, hurling sizzling and hissing hailstones against the cottage window panes. I love these wild winter nights.

I believe in the close and regular observance of our natural world. I have always gleaned intense pleasure just wandering around my garden and, whenever possible, the surrounding fields, woods, moorlands and hedgerows. My attitude is extremely casual and I am far removed from the well-read botanist, naturalist or informed gardener. In Edward Thomas's writing:

> *No matter what the weather, on earth,*
> *At any age between death and birth, –*
> *To see what day or night can be*
> *The sun and the frost, the land and the sea,*
> *Summer, Autumn, Winter, Spring, –*

I recognize an echo of my very philosophy on life.

I must have the blood of the Cornish wreckers coursing through my veins for I just love to plunder the spoils of a good storm. Along the seashore and hedgerows, in the deciduous woods and the pine thickets, over the moorland and in the garden there are treasures galore. In fact, if it was not for our stormy weather I would never have discovered some of the exciting natural bits and pieces that I use in my collages.

The storms have wrenched a great variety of lichens from the uppermost branches of the trees and all can be gathered, dried and used to decorate collages, scent potpourris and embellish botanical arrangements. The lichen-covered branches and twigs that come down are complete works of art in their own right.

Everyone who visits Cornwall must be aware of the beautiful lichens that festoon and adorn every tree, shrub, wooden fence and gate, wall and boulder. In my garden alone there is such a rich diversity. I can amuse myself for hours by walking through the countryside feasting my eyes on the tendrils, fronds, frills, pucker-ings, smockings, clottings and coatings of lichen. I love their colors which change with the humidity, as do their texture and their pen-dant state. The textured surfaces of some of the flat lichens are like pale almond-green, gray and even black bubbling pancakes. Some-times their surfaces are powdered in the palest green.

Many of the more substantially fronded lichens are fragrant. One such lichen, known as oakmoss (what a confusing name for a lichen), has the perfume of musk-lavender which is stronger if the lichen is very dry. Others, particularly a few of the very prolific hairlike varieties, smell of antiseptic and this smell is more powerful when the lichen is sodden.

This garland is quite exquisite, particularly if you look closely at the delicate sea-green web of filaments. It is photographed in a long-deserted farmyard on a turquoise painted barn door.

LICHEN GARLAND

*A*FTER a recent storm I collected armfuls of this wonderful hair-like lichen. A large tree was blown onto its side and the lichen was scattered everywhere, some still attached to broken branches and some strewn over the lane. I gathered small festooned branches and loose lichen knowing that it would be unusual and beautiful used in botanical arrangements or for decorating winter garlands.

☙ Wrap lichen around a homemade vine base using rubber cement to keep any straggling fronds tucked in place.

☙ Lichen is so beautiful and unusual that it may well not be necessary to add anything else to the garland other than the tartan bows which are tied at intervals around the wreath and help to keep the lichen in place.

The felt bracelet was made in the 1930s. I clearly remember my mother sitting with her nail scissors snipping away at pieces of felt and fashioning them into the most charming flowers and leaves. This photograph is taken on the coffin bridge over the stream and it was, at one time, the only means of crossing the Trethellan Water other than fording. The purple stripes in the tartan rug are exactly the color of some of the more unusual purple anemones.

CORNISH ANEMONES ON A TARTAN RUG

*T*HERE is no other flower that possesses such a vibrant and rich range of colors as do anemones. The beautiful lipstick reds, blues, purples and carmines and the occasional white streaked with green anemone are quite stunning. They are invaluable in my work whether pressed, dried in silica gel or used fresh. The anemones are displayed in an old royal blue enamel French saucepan, where I feel their flamboyant but nonetheless homely beauty looks quite at ease.

By banding the flowers together in their original bundles they remain upright but still appear uncontrived.

In fact, because of the aromatic and preservative qualities of some lichens, they were frequently used by the ancient Egyptians to stuff the cranial cavity of their embalmed ancestors. Oakmoss has been used for this purpose, and it is still used in the making of perfume. The fragrant oil contained in this lichen also has fixative properties ensuring that a perfume retains its fragrance over a long period. What a fascinating history to a demure-fronded lichen that grows so freely in my garden.

Pine cones, too, came tumbling from their perches during the gales, and today I found some huge specimens. The immature cones are still attached to their branches and some look like smooth fossils while others are ridged and decorated with both fronded and flat lichens. What a find! I think this must be the first time I have been able to examine closely the great immature cones occasionally seen perched high in massive pine trees towering 100 feet or more into the skies. In addition, the storms have thrown lots of interesting and more unusual seaweeds, shells, skeletal remains and driftwood onto the shoreline, as well as the great ropes and bundles of twine which I have yet to find a use for! Mosses, too, have hurtled from roofs and trees. If they can be retrieved all the better, but I tend to gather my mosses from the stones, tree trunks and the sheltered, dank places of the garden, about which George Meredith wrote so perceptively when he said,

> *Still as the mosses that glow*
> *Over the flooring and over the lines*
> *Of the roots here and there.*

I find these mosses quite as exquisite as the lichens and I enjoy using them in all my work. Some of the coarser mosses look like iridescent-emerald chenille wool, others are pads of virescent silk velvet, scraps of olive-green felt, thick sponges of apple-green fibers, little pelted mats of green threads and even orange-whiskered plump viridian cushions. In fact, the orange-whiskered cushions have established themselves on the ridge tiles of the cottage roof and standing on the high bank at the back of the cottage the roof has the most appealing bewhiskered appearance. All the mosses and lichens must be dried flat in a warm place. They can be pressed but it is a great pity to flatten them; if you wish to create a flat collage then just press them lightly. Seaweeds must be rinsed several times in cold water and then, after dabbing dry, pressed in the usual manner, changing the paper daily until the fronds are quite dry.

Driftwood and lichen-covered branches should be dried in a warm place for at least a week before being displayed.

The Trethellan Water, tributary to the beautiful River Kennall, in early winter. Home to countless trout, moorhen and coot, water vole and silver-tummied water shrew and the hunting ground of the heron. Peaty and brown after heavy rain our river can flood the lower garden and road dramatically, the waters subsiding just as quickly as they rise.

The evenings are imperceptibly lengthening, and when the sun emerges from its usual blanketting of cloud it is warm. The crowds of pretty snowdrops that bob and flirt in the wind respond in minutes to the winter sunshine, shedding their dewy mantle and opening their three outer petals to reveal a delicate, green-tipped inner bell exquisitely perfumed with the mossy scent of bluebells. Close companion to the snowdrops is the delicate, lilac-flowered *Crocus Tomasinianus*, whose yellow-stamened center is perfumed with the softest reminder of the wild flowers of spring. The marbled leaves of the celandine are lying flat against the mossy soil. Haw, green and gold finches are feeding quite close to the cottage, as is the little Jenny wren.

Our robin appears as soon as I am in the garden, and the blackbirds and house sparrows are becoming quite noisy. I think that the crows have started nesting and the visiting winter birds are less in evidence. The air around the pond is filled with the sweet, spicy perfume of the white-flowered water hawthorn and floating around the blossoms are great masses of frogs' eggs. The leaves of the Caucasian marsh marigold (or kingcup) are emerging from the water and uncurling their large fleshy parasols. In the luxury of the rich afternoon sun,

> the winter's cheek flushed as if he had drained
> Spring, Summer and Autumn at a drought
> And smiled quietly.

EDWARD THOMAS

It illuminates the orange-scarlet shoots of the scarlet willow and the egg-yolk yellow of the golden willow.

Our moist garden is a paradise for willows and I grow as many varieties as I can. The colors and shapes of willow catkins are extremely diverse and I have black-furred, flesh-pink, and silver-furred catkins, plump gray ones, tiny white catkins, yellowish silver-haired catkins, brick-red catkins and many more besides. Shoots of these willows, brought into the house in early winter, will produce their catkins after only a few days and I enjoy having a large jug of mixed willows in the sitting room. Not only will they produce their catkins, but ultimately roots as well, providing young plants for the garden and for friends. Slender shoots of catkin-adorned willow press beautifully and all catkins can be picked, dried and used as interesting and unusual additions to potpourris.

A tuft of the lichen Pseudevernia furfuracea *growing in the chink of a granite wall.*

MOSS-COVERED BASKET
OF DRIED FLOWERS

*H*AVING very little room in the cottage to store all my dried flowers I decided that, rather than keep them in numerous odd boxes, I would put them all in one huge old basket. I put all botanicals of a kind together and tied them in manageable bunches. Sheaves of marjoram, tiny bunches of quaking and common bent grass, woodrush, thistles, teazles, yarrow, centaurea, alliums and a host of old roses, hydrangeas, cynara, cotton lavender and anything that had caught my eye were packed, cheek by jowl, into their newfound home. Looking at their lovely colors, almost as bright as the day I gathered them, I had the idea that they would look even lovelier in a deep, rich green "mossy" basket.

Gather together dried mosses and patch them onto a basket, just lightly brushing the back of the pads of moss with rubber cement. When you tire of such a green basket, simply pull the moss off, for the rubber cement is easily pulled away from any surface.

Any container could be covered in moss. A deep wooden crate, sturdy cardboard box or even a plastic container serves the purpose just as well. If a paler effect is desired, try using lichen or a mixture of moss and lichen.

The first warm-gold stars are flickering in the skies as I walk down the lane. Clouds on the eastern horizon are suffused with copper, and as the light slips away, the pale river ripples silver and black. The stars turn to silver, the moon brightens in the night sky, and violet-purple clouds curdle the western horizon. The river is swollen, and from the waterfalls there are deep subterranean gurgles as well as the more usual rushings. The feathered branches of the Monterey pines push their uppermost traceries into the frostings of the gathering Milky Way, and along the ridge of the valley hangs the plow, its handle pointing toward earth.

The church bells, muffled by the valley slopes, drift in and out of my consciousness. Climbing up the hill and out of the valley the bells become thunderous, their pealing emanating from the weatherworn Norman churchtower. From within, a light shines through the rich colors of the chancel window, and in the church-yard the great bare sycamores house the now-silent rooks. The white- and ocher-lichened gravestones peep above the wall as I pass, dipping and bobbing in unison with my homeward gait.

Turning off the road and over the stile my footsteps are hushed by the soft ground. The path follows the high backbone of Cornwall and the air is cold and sharp against my face. Turning down into our valley I am welcomed back by its softer air and the silver music of the river. Looking around the garden, dappled by the shadows cast by the moon, my thoughts turn to the making of a moonlight garden. The flowers of dusk and night are pale, languid beauties. Their petals have no veining for they have no need to attract the bee. Almost all are exquisitely perfumed for they rely on the night-flying moths for pollination. Some of these flowers release their perfume as soon as their petals open, and the fragrance hangs in the air until the flower has been fertilized, when often the sweet smell turns fetid. Others release their perfume in intermittent puffs, possibly to conserve the strength of their fragrance. Jasmine, wild night-flowering catchfly, evening primrose, night-scented stocks and sweet rocket are just a few of the more common, sweetly scented flowers of the dusk and night. They could all be planted in a moonlight garden, together with other pale-flowered and pale-leaved plants. Honeysuckle will project a stronger per-fume at night and together with jasmine, it could twine over a white-painted trellis. Of course, a beautiful pale stone statue would complete such a moonlight garden.

Our tulip tree is only a few years old but it is already encrusted with mosses and lichens. This green, hair-like moss is beautiful when dried and used in collages as are, of course, the lovely almond-green lichens and the crumpled pewter-grey ones.

Now is the time to search the woodland floor and garden for skeletonized leaves. If there is a magnolia tree in the garden then almost certainly there will be skeletonized leaves beneath it. They are by far the most perfect to be found in any quantity, and I enjoy using them to create atmospheric backgrounds to many of my collages. I have also discovered that green magnolia leaves can be gathered from the tree and skeletonized by pressure cooking them in about 1–1½ inches of water, to which has been added one teaspoon of soda crystals, for about twelve minutes. If the tissue of the leaves still cannot be brushed away from the skeletons after the cooking time, then they will need a further five to ten minutes in the pressure cooker which should do the trick.

Few people are aware of just how beautiful flowers of the edible carrot are. I discovered them quite by accident when I left unharvested carrots in the soil of our coldframe throughout one winter. As the warmer weather of late winter arrived, so the carrots started to sprout their lovely green foliage. I left them in place over the summer, occasionally picking some leaves to press and also using them in spring and summer flower arrangements. By August, my carrot plants were about 4 feet tall and profusely covered in beautiful umbels of almond-green and white flowers. They are by far the loveliest of the umbelliferous blossoms to press and out-standingly dainty in fresh flower arrangements.

I have since discovered that any shop-bought carrots nor-mally used for cooking can be planted in the winter months for flowering in the summer. I would recommend growing a large pot of them in the greenhouse or a sunny window, or just a clump of five or six in a coldframe. If you want to grow them in the open garden, then the whole carrots should be planted after the fear of frosts has passed.

Suet Pudding has settled quite happily into the family, cot-tage and garden. She is a wonderful huntress and each day, much to my dismay, she brings home game for the family's supper. We all adore her, except Ebony, who continually ambushes her from all sides, breaking all the rules of honorable battle. They both love to look around the garden with me, when there is an instant role reversal, as Suet ambushes Ebony. Perhaps Ebony will soon capitu-late to Suet's immense charm and tolerance. After all, who could resist the thought of a woodsy garden shared with a friend who will catch your breakfast, lunch and supper?

Last night, a bright full moon cast sharp shadows across our bedroom floor and I lay listening to the metallic bark of a dog fox echo through a garden as light as day. In the twilight hours, the high-pitched warbling of our robin heralded the thinnest morning chorus, the first of the season. Soon the whole garden will reverberate with birdsong during those early moments, and I will become accustomed to its beauty and listen with only half an ear as I drift in and out of sleep. The morning clouds are frilled and flounced in apricot satin, and gawky, long-stemmed snowdrops, exquisite purple hellebores, bright blue pulmonaria, wild primroses and early daffodils bask in the early sun. At the back of the cottage, the celandines are opening their yellow enameled petals and the smell of their juicy stems takes me back to the orchard where as a child I first picked them. A breeze ruffles the daffodils and in the warming sun the first tattered butterfly weakly flutters over the leafless rose bushes of the terrace. The skylarks are singing, flurries of gnats dance in the sunshine, a bee flies straight into my face and I know that spring is with us. The year has turned full circle, never altering for a moment its ancient rythmn, and soon I will be ravished by the cow parsley flooding our lanes; by the blackthorn blossom against blue skies; by the smell of primroses and spotted cowslips, and by the new green leaves, just as I always have been and always will be. If the music of the spheres can be heard, it must surely be when winter turns to spring.

> *In the pale sunshine, with frail wings unfurled*
> *Comes to the bending snowdrop the first bee,*
> *She gives her winter honey prudently;*
> *And faint with travel in a bitter world,*
> *The bee makes music, tentative and low,*
> *And spring awakes and laughs across the snow.*
>
> MARY WEBB

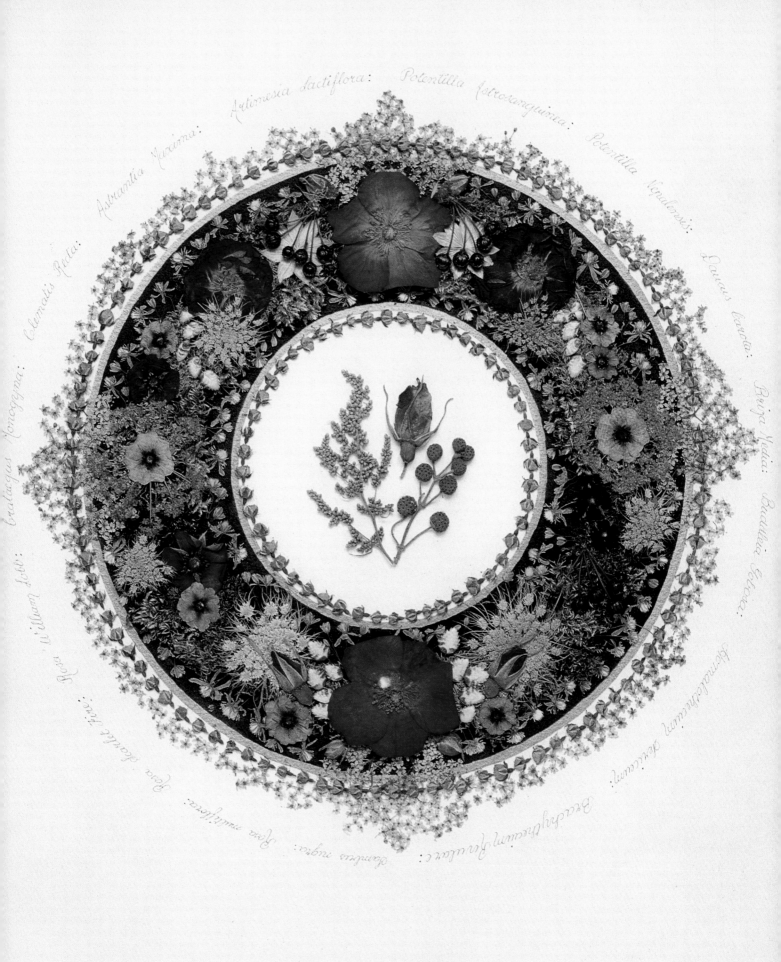

PRESSING AND DRYING PLANTS

PRESSING

All pressed botanicals should be dried as quickly as possible. With few exceptions, they will then retain their original colours.

Layer flowers, leaves, berries, sliced fruits and vegetables (and occasionally small whole ones), or anything else which takes your fancy between one-way *smooth* diaper liners (some liners are textured and will leave botanicals with a waffled surface). Then place this inside either a folded large sheet of newspaper or recycled paper. Two separate, smaller sheets do just as well.

Each sheet of botanicals should then be layered between a further three sheets of folded paper or six single sheets, before being placed in the press. This allows plenty of paper for absorption of the moisture drawn from the botanicals.

Replace the empty sheets of paper between the sheets of botanicals every 24 hours. Either fresh paper can be used or the existing paper dried over a radiator. Continue doing this until the botanicals are dry and crisp. This is of crucial importance and ensures that everything dries quickly and retains its color.

Thin flowers and leaves take four or five days; plumper flowers and buds a week or more, and some vegetables and fruit (particularly juicy slices) two to three weeks.

HANG DRYING

A great variety of flowers, leaves, seedheads and cones can be hang dried, tied in bunches using strips cut from stockings which stretch around the stems without cutting into them.

Hang the bunches upsidedown in a warm spot.

If colors are to remain bright, speed is of the essence. The ideal place is above a radiator or boiler, or in an airing cupboard. Experiment with almost everything, but be prepared for shrinkage as botanicals reduce in size by about two-thirds of their original size.

FLAT DRYING

Many single blossoms, double flowers and all petals flat dry well. Placed on sheets of newspaper in a warm spot, they slowly dessicate to only a fraction of their original size, but their texture is delightful.

SILICA GEL DRYING

Most flowers dry perfectly in silica gel crystals, keeping their color, shape and size extremely well. Place an inch layer of silica gel in the bottom of a container, wedge the blossoms in it upright and gently pour more crystals over them until they are completely covered. Take care to fill all gaps. If there is room, a further layer of blossoms can be added, covered in the same way. Position sprays of flowers sideways, which enables them to keep their shape. Cover them with crystals very slowly.

Seal the container with an airtight cover and leave for two or three days. To empty the container, tip it sideways and carefully remove the botanicals as they are freed of the silica gel. If they are not crisp and dry, replace them in the crystals for a day or two. By regularly drying out the crystals in a lukewarm oven, they retain their power of dessication.

. . . .

ABOVE
Mentha buddleiafolia *and yellow*
Lysimachia ciliata.
OPPOSITE
With its repetitive geometric design, this picture evokes the divine order of succession within the garden.

All things began in order, so shall they end, and so shall they begin again; according to the ordainer of order and mystical mathematicks of the City of Heaven.

The Garden of Cyrus

142

A SEASONAL GUIDE TO SUITABLE PLANTS FOR PRESSING AND DRYING

Each season there is so much to gather from the garden and countryside. The following is a guide to my favourites with an indication as to the best way to dry each one. All manner of botanicals can be pressed and dried – experiment with whatever takes your fancy.

Key
D = *hang dry*
P = *press*
S = *silica gel dry*

FLOWERS

SPRING

Akebia (P)
American currant (P)
Blackthorn (P)
Bluebells (D,P)
Bridal wreath (P)
Buttercups (P)
Celandines (P)
Columbines (P)
Campions (P)
Comfrey (P)
Crab apple (P)
Cherry (P)
Cow parsleys (P)
Daisies (P)
Dandelions (P)
De Caen anemones (D,P)
Euphorbia (P)
Forget-me-nots (P)
Grape hyacinths (D,P)
Herb Robert (P)
Hellebores (D,P)
Japonica (P)
Jacob's Ladder (P)
Kingcups (D,P)
Laburnum (P)
Lady's smock (P)
Lilac (D,P)
Periwinkles (P)
Primroses (P)
Pulmonaria (P)
Sweet Cicely (P)
Violets (P)
Wisteria (P)
Woodruff (P)

SUMMER

Alchemilla mollis (D,P)
Anaphalis (D,P)
Aruncus sylvester (D,P)
Astilbe (D,P)
Carrots (P)
Clematis (D,P)
Daisies (P)
Delphinium (D,P)
Deutzia (P)
Docks (D,P)
Geraniums (D,P)
Goat's rue (P)
Hawthorn (P)
Hostas (P)
Irises (P)
Jacob's ladder (P)
Larkspur (D,P)
Lady's bedstraw (D,P)
Lavender (D,P)
Lilac (P)
Meadowsweet (D,P)
Pansies (P)
Pelargoniums (P)
Polygonum campanulatum (P)
Potentilla (D,P)
Reseda (P)
Rosebay willowherb (P)
Roses (D,P)
Sorrel (P)
Syringa (D,P)
Yarrow (D,P)

AUTUMN

Acanthus (D)
Anaphalis (D,P)
Aconitum carmichaelii (D,P)
Anemones, Japanese (P)
Artemisia lactiflora (P)
Borage (P)
Burnet (D,P)
Buddleia (D,P)
Cardoons (D)
Cosmos atropurpurea (P)
Clematis species (D,P,S)
Eryngiums (D)
Feverfew (D,P)
Fleabane (P)
Fuchsia (P,S)
Hydrangeas (D,P)
Hops (D,P)
Pansies (P)
Polemonium (P)
Polygonum campanulatum, pink and white varieties (D,P)
Potentillas (D,P)
Stattice (D)
Violas (P)
Yarrow (D,P)

WINTER

Aconites (P)
Anemones, de Caen (P,S)
Brunnera macrophylla (P)
Celandines (P)
Comfrey (P)
Crocuses (D,P)
Heathers (D,P)
Mahonia japonica (P)
Daisies (P)
Narcissus, Soleil d'Or (S,P)
Pansies (P)
Periwinkles (P)
Primroses (P)
Pulmonaria (P)
Snowdrops (P)
Water hawthorn (D,P)

LEAVES

SPRING

Conifer shoots(P)
Ferns, uncurling and open (D,P)
Tree leaves, newly emerging (P)

SUMMER

Alchemilla conjuncta (P)
Carrot (D,P)
Contorted rush (D,P)
Docks (D,P)
Ferns (D,P)
Hostas (P)
Selinum tenufolium (P)

AUTUMN

Conifer sprigs (D,P)
Ivy (P)
Olearia in variety (P)

WINTER

Abutilon (P)
Acer (P)
American currant (P)
Bracken (P)
Burnet (P)
Ferns (P)
Geraniums (P)
Ivy (P)
Malus (P)
Parrotia (P)
Potentilla (P)
Prunus (P)
Tellima (P)
Vines (P)

HERBS

SPRING

Sprouting shoots (P)

SUMMER

Angelica (D)
Aromatic leaves (D,P)
Elecampane (D)
Fennel (P)
Feverfew (D,P)
Lovage (P)
Marjoram (D,P)
Mint (D,P)
Sage (P)
Smallage (P)
Thyme (D,P)

AUTUMN

Artemisias in variety (D,P)
Chamomile, single and double (D,P)
Fennel (D,P)
Marjoram (D,P)
Mints, in variety (D,P)
Rue (P)
Sage (D,P)

Santolina (D,P)
Thyme (D,P)
Vervain (P)

WINTER

Rosemary (P)
Rue (P)
Sage (P)

SEEDHEADS

SUMMER

Columbine (D,P)
Cotoneaster (P)
Pyracantha (P)

AUTUMN

Astilbes (D)
Cardoons (D)
Centaurea (D)
Docks (D,P)
Chinese lanterns (D)
Eryngiums (D)
Honesty (D)
Love-in-a-mist (D)
Meadowsweet (D,P)
Poppies (D)
Sea carrot (D)
Teazle (D)

WINTER

Cynara (D)
Eryngiums in variety (D)
Iris sibirica (D)

VEGETABLES AND FRUITS

SPRING

Alfalfa sprouts (P)
Beans in variety (P)
Citrus fruits (D)
Fennel (P)
Kiwi fruit (P)
Lychees (D)
Mangetout peas (P)
Mushrooms (P)
Okra (P)
Parsley (P)
Red cabbage (P)
Strawberries (P)

SUMMER

Peas, young pods (P)
Beans, young pods (P)

Carrot, tiny whole and sliced (P)
Tropical fruits, tiny whole and sliced (P)
Tropical vegetables, tiny whole and sliced (P)
Strawberries, alpine (P)
Strawberries, large, sliced (P)
Sweetcorn, small (D,P)

AUTUMN

As spring

WINTER

As spring

MISCELLANEOUS

SPRING

Alder cones, new (P)
Fir cones (D)
Mosses and lichens, in variety (D,P)
Scented woods from pruning (D)
Seaweeds (P)
Willow catkins (D,P)

SUMMER

Alder cones, new (D)
Conifer, small new cones (D,P)
Grasses (D,P)
Mosses and lichens, in variety (D,P)
Scented woods (D)
Seaweeds (P)

AUTUMN

Alder cones (D)
Blackberries, immature (P)
Bracket fungus (D,P)
Catkins (D,P)
Cotoneaster berries (D,P)
Gourds (D)
Grasses (D,P)
Mushrooms, field (P)
Pumpkins (D)
Pyracantha berries (D,P)
Rose hips (D,P)
Rowan berries (D,P)
Toadstools, non-poisonous (P)

WINTER

Alder cones (P,D)
Berries, in variety (D,P)
Catkins (D,P)
Fir cones (D)
Liriodendron wood (D)
Mosses and lichens in variety (D,P)
Oak apples (D)
Pine, sawdust and chippings (D)
Rose hips (D,P)
Scented woods (D)
Seaweed in variety (P)

ROSES

The following roses are of particular value, but almost all the old-fashioned ones can be used in one way or another. Dry all roses that are highly fragrant, either whole or just the petals, and use them in pot pourri. Visually, the best ones are the dark red roses, particularly the Damask rose and 'Roseraie de l'Hay'. Rose petals are best dried flat on sheets of newspaper in a warm place.

'Apothecary's Rose' *(R. gallica)* (D,P)
'Cecile Brunner' (D,P)
Damask rose *(R. damascena)* (D)
'Kiftsgate' (P)
R. multiflora (P)
Provence rose *(R. centifolia)* (D)
'Provins rose' (D)
'Rosa Mundi' *(R. gallica)* (D,P)
'Roseraie de l'Hay' (D)
'Scarlet Fire' (P)
Threepenny-bit rose *(R. farreri persetosa)* (P)
'Veilchenblau' (D,P)

COMMON PLANTS AND THEIR SCIENTIFIC NAMES

Most of the plants in the text are referred to by their common name. Here is a list of the scientific names for the wild plants should you wish to find out more about them.

alkanet *Anchusa officinalis*
alpine strawberry *Fragaria vesca*
barrenwort *Epidemedium alpinum*
bellflower *Campanula* spp.
bindweed *Convolvulus arvensis*
birthwort *Artistolochia longa*
blackberry *Rubus fruticosus*
bladderwort *Utricularia* spp.
bluebell *Endymion non-scriptus*

bogbean *Menyanthes trifoliata*
bouncing Bet *Sapinaria officinalis*
campion *Silene dioca*
catchfly *Lychnis* spp.
Caucasian kingcup *Caltha polypetala*
celandine *Ranunculus ficaria*
Chinese lantern *Physalis alkekengi*
cockscomb *Celosia argentea*
comfrey *Symphytium* spp.
common meadow-rue *Thalictrum flavum*
cowbane *Cicuta virosa*
cow parsley *Anthriscus sylvestris*
cowslip *Primula veris*
crab apple *Malus sylvestris*
cranesbill *Geranium* spp.
creeping Jenny *Lysimachia nummularia*
dame's violet *Hesperis matronalis*
dog violet *Viola riviniana*
drimys *Drimys winteri*
elecampane *Inula helenium*
evening primrose *Oenothera* spp.
figwort *Scrophularia* spp.
fleabane *Pulicaria dysenterica*
foxglove *Digitalis purpurea*
grape hyacinth *Muscari atlanticum*
harebell *Campanula rotundifolia*
heartsease *Viola tricolor*
henbane *Hyoscyamus niger*
herb Bennet *Geum urbanum*
herb Robert *Geranium robertianum*
honesty *Lunaria biennis*
horehound, black *Ballota nigra*
horehound, white *Marrubium vulgare*
houndstongue *Cynoglossum officinale*
Jacob's ladder *Polemonium caeruleum*
joe-pye weed *Eupatorium cannabinum*
lad's love *Artemisia abrotanum*
lady's bedstraw *Galium verum*
lady's smock *Cardamine pratensis*
lesser spearwort *Ranunculus flammula*
lily of the valley *Convallaria majalis*
lungwort *Pulmonaria officinalis*

mallow *Malva* spp.
mare's tail *Hippuris vulgaris*
marsh marigold *Caltha palustris*
meadowsweet *Filipendula ulmaria*
Michaelmas daisy *Aster novi-belgii*
milkwort *Polygala* spp.
monkshood *Aconitum napellus*
myrtle *Myrico gale*
parrot weed *Myriophyllium proserpinacoides*
pennywort *Hydrocotyle vulgaris*
periwinkle *Vinca* spp.
poke weed *Phytolacca americana*
primrose *Primula* spp.
ragged robin *Lychnis flos-cuculi*
rosebay willowherb *Epilobium angustifolium*
roseroot *Rhodiola rosea*
sedges *Carex* spp.
sheep's bit scabious *Jasione montana*
sneezewort *Achillea ptarmica*
snowdrop *Galanthus nivalis*
sorrel *Rumex* spp.
speedwell *Veronica* spp.
staunchwort *Achillea millefolium*
stitchwort *Stellaria* spp.
stock *Matthiola* spp.
sweet briar *Rosa rubiginosa*
sweet Cicely *Myrrhis odorata*
sweet flag *Acorus calamus*
sweet rocket *Hesperis matronalis*
sweet woodruff *Galium odoratum*
valerian *Valleriana* spp.
viper's bugloss *Echium vulgare*
water avens *Geum rivale*
water hemlock *Oenathe crocata*
water mint *Mentha aquatica*
Welsh poppy *Meconopsis cambrica*
white ragged robin *Lychnis flos-cuculi*
wild hop *Humulus lupulus*
willowherb *Epilobium* spp.
wolfsbane *Aconitum vulgaris*
yarrow *Achillea millefolium*
yellow pimpernel *Lysimachia nemorum*

Page numbers in italics indicate photographs

A

144

Aconitum carmichaelii, 102, 114, *115*
akebia 19, 93
alders 12, 16, 93
aliums 44, 135, *135*
alkanet 63, 64
anaphalis *66–7*, 68, *116*
anemones 85, 132, *132*
angelica, 43, 56, 98
   A. archangelica 56
anthericums 63
artemesias 48
arum lilies 16, *49*
Arundo donax 88
astilbe 7, *66–7*, 68, 69
astrantias 48–52, 98
Aulacomnium andrognum 8
avens, water 62
azaleas *10–11*, 12

B

balsam, white 72
bamboos, 44, 70
bane family 20
bellflower 63
bergamot 48
betony, white 62
bindweed 125
birthwort 21
blackberries 93
blackthorn 16, 29, 36, 80, 108, 118
blinks, water 35
bluebells 6, 18, 38, 40, 42, 44, 104, 125, 134
bouncing Bet 84
bracken 104, 125
bryony 6
buddleia *66–7*, 68, 72
   B. globosa 48
bugloss, viper's 20
buttercups 43, 52

C

camelias 12
campanulas 12
campions 16, *18*, 38, 40, 43, 48, 63, 64, 93, 125
carrot, flower 137
catchfly 136
catkins 134
celandines 16, 138
centaurea 135, *135*
cherry, wild 118
Chinese lanterns 89, *89*
cimicifugas 102
clematis 7, *66–7*, 68, 93
   C. armandii 19
   C. durandii 52, *66–7*, 68
   C. montana 25
   C. recta 110, *111*
   C. tanguitica 100, *101*
   C. viticella 110, *111*
cock's comb 89, *89*
columbine 48, 104, 125
comfrey 35, 43, *53*, 63, 64, 125
convolvulus 93
cornus 12
Cosmos atrosanguineus 66–7, 68, 102, 110, *111*
cotoneaster berries 86, *87*

cotton lavender *72*, 73, 135, *135*
cow parsley 18, 43, 44, 110, *111*, 118, 125
cowslips 19, 138
   Himalayan 69
cranesbill 104
creeping Jenny 63
crocosmias 102
Crocus Tomasinianus 134
cyclamen 84
cynara 135, *135*
cyperus flowers *72*, 73
Cyperus alternifolius 88
cyprus 12

D

daffodils 6, 35, 80, 138
Dahlia merckii 102
daisies 16, 125
dame's violet 36, 44, 63
dandelions 35, 125
datura 78
day lilies *17*
deadly nightshade 6
deutzia 63
dicentra 125
Dicentra spectabilis 35
dog violets 16
   white 62
dog daisies 44
double lady's smock 37
drimys 93

E

elder flowers 44
   leaves 9
elecampane 98
Eryngium lassauxii 102, *103*
eucalyptus 9
euphorbias 35
Euphorbia melifera 48
evening primrose 136

F

fatsia 93
ferns *8*, *10–11*, 31, 38, 44, 48, *62*, 63, 64, 80, 104
   crested 62
   maidenhair 37, *37*, *53*
   Royal *17*
feverfew 128, *128*
figwort, 63
flag iris 43
flag, sweet 93, 98
fleabane 21, 72, 102
Florentine iris 98
forget-me-nots 36
foxgloves 48, 64
fritillaria 31
Fritillaria meleagris 35
fuchsias 71

G

garlic, wild 36
geraniums *43*
   G. macrorrhizum 98
   G. pratense 52
   G. procurrens 69
grape hyacinth 19, 35
grasses, 39, *39*, 44, 70, *98*, 135, *135*
gunnera *28*, 69, 104, 118

H

hawkweed 62
hawthorn 6, 16, 36, 48, 93, 104, 118
hazel 118
   contorted 56
heartsease 125
heathers 125
hellebores *31*, 129
Hellebores viridis 125
hemlock 6, 78
henbane 78
Hensol harebell 48, 52
herb Bennet 98
herb Robert 16, 40, 44, 62
honesty 19, 36, 125
honeysuckle *72*, 93, 118, 136
hop 88
horehound 48
hostas *10–11*, 35, 44
hound's-tongue 20
hydrangeas 7, 81, *81*, 135, *135*
Hydrangeas paniculata 81

I

Inula hookeri 69
irises *10–11*
   I. kaempferi 17
   I. sibirica 52, *66–7*, 68, 124, *125*
ivy 9, 19, 21, 48, *50*, 51, 71, *72*, 73, 93

J

Jacob's ladder 43, 44, 63
Japanese anemone 72
jasmine 136
joe-pye weed 48
juniper 93

K

kingcups *31*, 35, 40
   Caucasian 16
knaufia *66–7*, 68

L

lad's love 21
lady's bedstraw 48, 104
lady's mantle 7, 63
lavender 9, 128, *128*
libertia 36
lichen *66–7*, 68, *119*, 126, *126*, *127*, 130, 131, *131*, 133
lilac 44, *72*, 93
   'Sensation' 63
lily-of-the-valley 104
loosestrife, purple 69
love-in-a-mist *53*
lysimachias 7
Lysimachia ciliata 52
   L. clethroides 69

M

magnolia 37, *37*, 124, *125*, 137
mahonia 125
mallow 36, 110, *111*
mare's tail 63
marigold, Caucasian marsh 134
marjoram 62, 135, *135*
meadow rue, common 63
meadowsweet 7, 35
Michaelmas daisy 99
mimulus 56, 104

M. auranticus 56
   M. cardinalis 56
   M. moschatus 56
   M. ringens 56
mind-your-own-business *50*, 51
mints 7, *10–11*, *52*, 64
   giant 44
   water 9, 63
monkey flower 69
monkshood, 63, 78
mosses *53*, 69, 133
muehlenbeckia *72*, 73
musk flower 56
myrtle 6, 93

N

narcissus, Soleil d'Or 118–19
nerines 102
Nicotiana langsdorfii 102
nightshade 78

O

oak 12
oakmoss 100, 130, 133
orchids 43, 44, 104
orris root 93

P

pansies *50*, 51
parrotia leaves 86, *87*
pelargoniums 98
pennyworts *8*, 48, 80
periwinkles 35, 125
philadelphus 63
physalis 86, *87*
pimpernel, yellow 63
pines, Monterey 9, 21, 35
pinkbells 43
pinks 9
pitosporum 93
pokeberry 78
polemonium *66–7*, 68
Polygonum campanulatum 17, 69
poppies 6, 44, 89, *89*
   Welsh 125
potentillas *72*, 73, 110, *111*
primroses 6, 12, 25–9, 104, 113, 125, 138
primulas *10–11*, *17*, 44, 52
   bog 40
   P. 'Inverewe' 52
   P. sibthorpii 19
   P. vialii 66–7, 68
Prunus serrulata 'Schimidsu Sakura' 25
pulmonarias 35, 125

R

ragged robin 44, 62, 104
ransomes 36
ranunculas *10–11*
Ranunculus ledebourii 52
rhododendrons *10–11*, 12
Rhubarb 44, *10–11*
rocket, sweet 136
roses 9, 19, *53*, 65, *72*, 93, *96*, 97, 110, *111*, 135, *135*
   'Blairii No.2' 65
   'Blanc Double de Coubert' 65
   'Cecile Brunner' 65
   'Celeste' 65
   farreri persetosa 29
   filipes 'Kiftsgate' 89, *89*
   'Kiftsgate' 65

mundi 65
   'Raubritter' 65
   'Roseraie de l'Hay' *60*, 61, 65
   'Souvenir du Dr Jamain' 65
   'Threepenny-Bit' 29, *65*
   'Tour de Malakoff' 65
   'William Lobb' 65
   'Veilchenblau' 65
roseroot 98
rowan 6, 80, 118
rushes 44
   contorted 56
   contorted spikes 63

S

sage 48
   wood 62
Sanguisorba canadensis 17
scabious *66–7*, 68
   sheep's bit, 48, 62, 93
   white field, 62
sea holly 124, *125*
sedges *62*, 63
skunk cabbage 35
sneezewort 21, 102
snowdrop 6, 16, 112, *112*, 113, *113*, 125
sorrel *18*, 43, 63, 64
   French, 48
   wood 63
spearwort, lesser 63
speedwell 16
spireas 7
spleenwort, maidenhair 129
Stipa gigantea 52
stitchwort 16, 38
stocks 6, 136
sunflowers 114, *114*, *115*
sweet briar 118
sweet Cicely 48, 98
sycamore 16

T

teazles 135, *135*
tellima 125
thalictrums 52
thistles 124, *125*, 135, *135*
thyme 9
   wild 62
tulip tree *136*

V

valerian, Pyrenean 63
vervain 56
viburnum 12
violets 6, 9, 35, 38, 104

W

water hemlock 48, *62*, 125
water hawthorn 35, 134
whitebells 43
willow herb, bog 63
   white rosebay 62
willows 12, 16, 69, 70, 125
   contorted 56
woodruff, sweet 36, 125
woodrush 35, 135, *135*
wort family 20

Y

yarrow 64, 93, 135, *135*
yew berries 6